D1462183

The Napoleonic Wars

A Captivating Guide to the Conflicts That Began Between the United Kingdom and France During the Rule of Napoleon Bonaparte and How They Stemmed from the French Revolution

Free Bonus from Captivating History (Available for a Limited time)

Hi History Lovers!

Now you have a chance to join our exclusive history list so you can get your first history ebook for free as well as discounts and a potential to get more history books for free! Simply visit the link below to join.

Captivatinghistory.com/ebook

Also, make sure to follow us on Facebook, Twitter and Youtube by searching for Captivating History.

Contents

Introduction

Today, France is regarded as not only the cultural capital of Europe but of that of the world as well. Generally regarded as a peaceful nation, it was not always so in French history other than that of the last 70 years, as France has always been one of the most militant countries in continental European history and strongly regarded as Europe's major military power since the Dark Ages. Though France had participated in both World War I and II, it lacked the military ingenuity and flair that have made the French stand out in some of the bloodiest conflicts in European military history including the Crusades. According to historian Niall Ferguson, "of the 125 major European wars fought since 1495, the French have participated in 50 – more than Austria (47) and England (43). Out of 168 battles fought since 387 BC, they have won 109, lost 49 and drawn 10," making France the most successful military power in European history—in terms of the number of battles fought and won.[1]

Since the fall of the Roman Empire, the French have always been in the thick of war, whether it be the Crusades, the Hundred Years' War, the Thirty Years' War, the War of Religion in the 16th century, or, even more recently, the First and Second World Wars. Even though the French military is no longer a major powerhouse like its United States or Chinese counterparts, the French Foreign Legion, a unilateral part of the French military, stands as one of the most active military branches and serves all across the globe.

The Napoleonic Wars, which took place between 1803 and 1815, were spearheaded by probably France's best tactician and military strategist to date, General Napoleon Bonaparte. His tactics and strategies were so grounded that it has served as the basis for many major warfare campaigns and maneuvers, both during his lifetime as well as after his demise. Even France's sworn enemy for most of the medieval era, the British, acknowledged his ingenuity despite his ultimate defeat at the hands of the British army at the end of life.

In this book, we will take an interesting journey through the annals of history to inspect the Napoleonic Wars: why they started in the first place, a glimpse into the life of the legendary commander Napoleon Bonaparte, the course of events and some of the major players on the board, and the stories of the last glimmer of France's military greatness. While the French Army did play a crucial role in both World Wars, they pale in comparison to the army of France, which was led by one of the most brilliant military minds in history, during the country's last great military campaign against its greatest rival, Britain. In this captivating book on the Napoleonic Wars and the French Revolution, we will examine Napoleon's role in the war not only as a military genius but also as a politician, ruler, and social reformer, and perhaps uncover some of the more dubious aspects of the legend that is Napoleon Bonaparte.

Chapter 1 – The French Revolution and Post-Revolution France

All historians on French history agree on the fact that Napoleon's campaigns were not that of a display of might and valor, which was still partially true, but the results of multiple events piling on one another since the bloody massacre known as the French Revolution. The French Revolution was the tipping point that tested and broke the patience of an entire nation burdened by war and famine. The monarch and the upper echelons of society feasted and drank merrily in their halls while the poor lay dying of starvation on the streets, the corpses piling up every day as the helpless victims of fate. A saying popularly quoted of a high-born noblewoman (usually identified as Queen Marie Antoinette despite lack of any concrete evidence), which is a popular favorite among many history teachers, is "If they can't eat bread, let them eat cake." Despite not knowing who this quote can be attributed to, it still shows how ignorant the upper-class and nobles were of the life and conditions of the general populace, who were mostly peasants and laborers overburdened by taxes that supported the incessant lavish lifestyle of their monarchs and the nobles.

The French Revolution occurred during the regime of King Louis XVI, the last of France's hedonistic monarchs whose administration was such a sheer and utter failure that it sparked a state of revolution within the nation for a little over ten years, beginning on May 5th, 1789 and ending on November 9th, 1799. The events that followed afterward not only affected France but the fate of its surrounding countries as well, starting the period known as the French Revolutionary Wars in the pages of history.

A lot of key factors were in play during the French Revolution and impacted the general state of the nation afterward which, when inherited by Napoleon Bonaparte, was forced to undertake a series of military conquests to ensure the existence and continued prosperity of the French nation. These factors included a mismanaged and crumbling economy that wasn't generating anything sustainable; a corrupt social system that forced people to step up for their rights, albeit in a bloody way; and a gradual change in the cultural values of the French lowborn society, which gave rise to the importance of the opinions of the masses instead of the opinions of the Church and kings.

All these factors turned the course of history in France, along with King Louis XVI's desperate attempts to lay more taxes on his subjects. He did this during the convention of the Estates General of 1789 in which he stripped Jacques Necker of his political power as the minister of finance due to Necker being a sympathizer of the commoners, the Third Estate, which helped to start the initial unrest. The Estates General was a general assembly where the monarchy, nobility, clergy, and the commoners were to come to one decision regarding state policies, but those policies always favored the nobility and the clergy, never the lower classes. Furthermore, the monarch decided to enlist the aid of military strength from neighboring allies, namely the German and the Swiss armies, for the convention of the Estates General, which only raised the tensions between the nobles and the commoners more. As usual, the king and his noblemen did nothing while the clergy delayed the convention, prompting the commoners to form the short-lived National Assembly. The main reason Necker was stripped of his post was because he gave a passionate three-hour speech on behalf of the commoners, which soon became the National Constituent Assembly after the events of Bastille Day.

Although the Estates General was comprised of commoners (the clergy and the nobility, the First and Second Estate, respectively, were also represented), it became clear that the latter two segments did not give much weight to the voice of the Third Estate, which ultimately led the commoners to doubt whether their grievances, which had lasted for decades, would ever be heard, if resolved, at all, leading to one of the darkest and most violent days in French history—Bastille Day. The National Assembly failed to gain the ear of the elites and the monarch, which prompted all-out mob fury. Emmanuel Joseph Sieyès, one of the key figures in the events of the coup of 18 Brumaire, incited the people with speeches and pamphlets, which brought them pouring into the streets while generating sympathy for Necker, who to them was the only honest public representative in the Estates General. When the news of Necker's dismissal on July 11th, 1789 circulated all throughout France, protests and violent unrest started erupting.

Though the revolutionaries were now under the control of the Bourgeois Militia of Paris, they had to seize weapons in order to exert control. So, on July 14, two days after the riots started, the revolutionaries in Paris aimed to take control of the Bastille, a lavish prison which was all but a fortress that housed the gunpowder they needed for the weapons they took from the Hôtel des Invalides. The prison housed only seven prisoners, who were all political prisoners that, at one time or another, had crossed King Louis XVI. What initially started out as a protest that surrounded the prison and called for its surrender turned into full-fledged mob fury when shots were fired. Representatives had been invited into the Bastille earlier in the day, and as the crowd continued to wait, they began to push closer in. Around 1:30 p.m., a group broke the chains on the drawbridge, causing a loud and sudden noise. As the soldiers called for the crowd to back away, the crowd, in the confusing chaos, took their shouts as encouragement to enter. Gunfire began to ring out, and this turned the crowd mad, as they thought they were being cornered like fish in a barrel. After 3 p.m., two canons arrived to back up the protesters so that the walls of the Bastille no longer offered viable protection to the defenders of the fort who had so far kept the crowd at bay. Bernard-René de Launay, the governor of the Bastille, called for a ceasefire around 5:00 p.m. While his conditions were refused, he still agreed to open the gates, and half an hour later, the fort was overtaken by the Bourgeois Militia of Paris. Three officers, along with de Launey, were executed by the crowd in their fury, leading to rumors of a revolt in the capital. However, the true horrors of the French Revolution were yet to come.

Though the Royal Army troops could have intervened, they had already shown their support for the people in a couple of events prior to the convention of the Estates General. In the following days, insurrection spread like wildfire across the nation, with the nobility starting to get executed and lynched by angry mobs all over France. Those who were lucky were able to flee successfully before the bloodbath really took a turn for the worse. The violence was bloody enough for the arrogant monarch to back down for the time being and who ultimately lost his power and privileges when the feudal social system that had been the basis of French society for ages was dissolved by the National Constituent Assembly, the assembly that had been formed by the previous National Assembly, between August 4th and 11th, 1789. The people were finally taking their rights back, and the abolishment of feudalism was just the start. The pre-revolution judiciary system was abolished as well, and the first constitution of France began to be worked on. Women also took their stand through the Women's March on Versailles on October 5th, which also resulted in another round of riots as the women of France demonstrated that they had had enough. The 7,000 women in the march broke through the palace gates, killing guards along the way, demanding for the king to end the food shortage and to make bread both cheap and plentiful. Another one of their demands was for the king to move his residence to Paris as a show of good faith in maintaining the balance of power with the common populace. Due to the violent nature of their protest, the king obliged to both demands.

Thus started France's first attempt at a constitutional monarchy, despite the arrogant and despotic nature displayed for hundreds of years by the nobility and the royal family. During these tumultuous times, France was the breeding ground for a diverse range of political ideologies which would forever change the political landscape of Europe for years to come. The failure at constitutional monarchy was due to Louis XVI's constant paranoia for his life and that of this family's, as well as the fact that he was constantly at odds with the bills proposed by the general assembly. In 1791, two years after the Bastille incident, the monarch and his surviving family members tried to escape to Austria on June 20th, historically referred to as the Royal Flight to Varennes. Ultimately, the escape resulted in failure when the king was recognized in Varennes, leading to his capture and return to Paris during which he and Queen Marie Antoinette were suspended of their royal rights and held in house arrest. The escape attempt was made just days before the constitution was about to be finalized, and it once again made the common populace dubious about the monarch's and the nobles' intent to keep their end of the agreement.

A small political turmoil followed after Jacques Pierre Brissot, a member of the General Assembly, drafted a petition demanding the monarch to be deposed for his unseemly act of cowardice. The seeds of dissent were further instigated by Georges Danton and Camille Desmoulins, who incited a mob that was confronted by the National Royal Guard led by Marquis de Lafayette, who, incidentally, was also a critical figure in the success of the Women's March to Versailles. Lafayette was an anomaly in all of these historic events— despite being an aristocrat by birth, he was a military hero who was much loved by the people of France and was a key player in not one but two major revolutions: the French Revolution and the July Revolution of 1830. One could safely say that before Napoleon's ascent to power, Lafayette was the most charismatic leader in France. Besides being an instrumental figure in two revolutions of his home country, he was also a key figure in improving the relationships between France and the newly formed United States of America. However, the key instigators of all this political turbulence at the time were the Jacobins, a particular group of political ideologists who are also generally considered responsible for the period known as the Reign of Terror when countless noblemen and noblewomen, along with large numbers of the clergy, were executed bloodily, introducing the world to the notorious guillotine. They were also the ones who lit the fire to the last straw of events that led to the decade-long French Revolutionary Wars, which saw France facing multiple hostile forces, repelling them all successfully.

This confrontation with the National Royal Guard led to a loss of civilian lives who were protesting for the petition to be signed. The Legislative Assembly was formed shortly after, ensuring that the people's rights were meted out properly with the monarchy needing to have the Assembly's say in all future decisions concerning the nation. Both the monarch and the Assembly had the power to veto the other's proposal, which soon turned out to be the root problem. King Louis XVI was not a man to back down easily and vetoed almost every proposal brought forth by the Assembly for nearly the next year. Many historians blame his childish ego of refusing to relegate power that was his birthright as the ultimate reason for the failure of the constitutional monarchy and the sad events that followed.

By August 1792, almost all of France was behind Jacques Pierre Brissot's original idea of overthrowing the monarchy since the constitutional monarchy proved to be ineffective due to both sides being unable to agree on anything properly. On August 10th, 1792, an angry crowd of commoners attacked the Tuileries Palace where the king and his family resided. Louis XVI was taken prisoner along with his family, and to avoid further chaos, the Legislative Assembly absolved the monarch's royal rights temporarily, suspending the monarchy. This led to the invasion of France by the Duke of Brunswick that started off with the siege of Longwy on August 19th. This was the beginning of the French Revolutionary Wars that lasted until 1802, the year prior to the beginning of the Napoleonic Wars.

Even though the monarchy was suspended and, theoretically, the revolution should have been over, the clash of the different political ideologies embroiled the nation into a civil war over the treatment of religion of the newly democratic France. The Catholic Church, which was the most powerful organization in Europe at that time, enjoyed a lot of privileges and exercised its actions without any form of accountability. The newly formed National Constituent Assembly (which lasted between July 1789 and September 1791) of France made sure that the people did not suffer due to the religious front, so they dismantled the traditional Catholic Church system in France and turned it into an accountable extension of the government by passing a law called the Civil Constitution of the Clergy in 1790. Two clauses of the bill caused monumental differences between the Church and the people partaking in the Revolution. The first was that clergymen were to be elected in their respective parishes by voting instead of being appointed by the Vatican, and the second stated that a patriotic oath would have to be taken by them prioritizing their loyalty to the nation and their fellow man over religion. These clauses essentially would break the Vatican's control over national affairs, which was one of the main reasons why the Church was a force that even monarchs and emperors avoided getting into conflicts with. The pope responded in kind by declaring all clergymen who accepted the Assembly's conditions as excommunicated, which led to the further fracturing of the nation. The clergymen split into two factions as a result—juring and non-juring, or refractory, priests. The former faction accepted the National Constituent Assembly's conditions to carry on their religious duties while the latter refused to do so.

Seven days into the Duke of Brunswick's invasion, peasants took over the French town of Vendee in response to the Legislative

Assembly's decree of deporting refractory priests to penal colonies like French Guinea, as they were considered as potential enemies of the nation in times of war. This didn't help the tensions being felt around the nation as rumors of political prisoners in Paris assisting the invading Prussian army were spread just days after the uprising of the peasants in Vendee, leading to a massacre of an estimated 1,500 prisoners in Paris between September 2nd and 4th, 1792. Most of these prisoners were priests, and the bloodbath that followed was unprecedented—most major towns and cities in France decided to follow with Paris' example and executed prisoners left and right, whether they were men of the cloth or common criminals.

The Battle of Valmy, which saw the Prussians attacking France but ended up being defeated on September 20th, 1792, played a significant role in bolstering the confidence of the revolutionaries who were on the verge of taking complete control of the government. It was a stunning victory for the French, who were led by General Kellerman and Dumouriez and who were aided by bad weather as well. The political instability of the country came to an end on September 20th when the first Democratic National Convention of France was formed, which overthrew the monarchy and permanently gave the power of the state to the people through elected representatives. By this time, the revolution had almost come to an end, but the embers of war that had been lit by the French Revolution was far from over.

Chapter 2 – The French Revolutionary Wars: A Divided Europe

The socio-political circumstances that led to the upheaval of the French Revolution combined with the sensitive religious sentiments set off the French Revolutionary Wars, which lasted from 1792 to 1802 and had started with Prussia's invasion of France. The main players in this decade-long era of war were Russia, Prussia, Austria, and Great Britain, although other nations were also involved. The French Revolutionary Wars are characterized by two phases—the War of the First Coalition and the War of the Second Coalition. The first phase lasted from 1792 to 1797, and the second phase took place between 1798 and 1802.

What happened in France on and following Bastille Day had all of Europe on its toes, with many countries that had a feudal society model outraged at how the common people took control of things during the French Revolution. But the following year saw a series of military campaigns end in disaster, starting with the one in Neerwinden. In this chapter, we will be discussing the First and Second Coalition Wars that had the newly born nation constantly under pressure before the war efforts were taken over by the larger-than-life hero of the Napoleonic Wars, Napoleon Bonaparte.

The War of the First Coalition

In actuality, though Prussia attacked France in 1792, the attack was the result of a series of political moves that were tied with the royal family, especially Queen Marie Antoinette's brother, Leopold II of Austria. Leopold II, who was also the emperor of the Holy Roman Empire, initiated the Declaration of Pillnitz on August 27th,1791. The declaration served as a warning letter for European monarchs to come together under a common cause before his sister or brother-in-law were harmed in any manner; however, this ultimately failed to save them when they were executed later in 1793. Eventually, after the Declaration of Pillnitz had been issued, France demanded that Austria remove all of its troops from their border as a defensive maneuver. The French monarchy had not been deposed as of yet, so Leopold II was evasive with his responses. This led the National Convention, the government that was formed after the Legislative Assembly disbanded in late September of 1792, to vote for declaring war against the Austrians, inciting the invasion from the Duke of Brunswick, Charles William Ferdinand. Even though the invasion was initially successful at Longwy and Verdun, the Prussian army faced a draw at the Battle of Valmy, and considering the upcoming winter and the mounting war expenses, the Prussian army backed down. The monarchy of France was formally abolished following this, which led to the French feeling emboldened by their actions. While this had been happening, the French had invaded the neighboring nations of Sardinia and Germany, eventually mounting a proper invasion against the Austrian Netherlands, taking over the country by the beginning of the following year of 1793.

But the tables turned that year when Spain, Holland, and Portugal joined the fray. The former king of France, Louis XVI, was killed shortly after those countries joined the anti-French coalition, which led to Britain entering the coalition. France began to employ the policy of mass conscription so they could fight on more fronts against such powerful enemies, but the early battles did not go very well.

The well-earned victory of the Austrian Netherlands campaign was reversed once the anti-French coalition launched the Flanders Campaign, and the allies were determined to crush the newly formed republic. What made things more complicated for France during this year were the revolts that broke out due to the civil war within the nation itself. Napoleon actually first distinguished himself in military affairs during this year by suppressing the dissent taking place in Toulon. He gained the reputation as an ingenious tactician after his tactical artillery placements succeeded in taking back the city without much loss of life or resources. The Jacobins had taken over the government by this point, suppressing internal dissents with brutal tactics which sparked the notorious Reign of Terror to begin in September, during which the former queen of France, Marie Antoinette, was executed later in October.

The year 1794 saw the French military return to form with multiple military victories occurring during the Flanders Campaign. General Jacques Coquille, more often referred to as Dugommier, is credited for keeping France safe from the invading Spanish forces; he not only defended French territory, but he also mounted a counterattack into the Spanish territory of Catalonia. His untimely death during the Battle of Sant Llorenç de la Muga, referred to as the Battle of the Black Mountain in English, halted the French incursion into the Spanish territory for the time being. Even though the French Army was enthusiastic, it lacked the advanced training and experience of the Spanish Army.

This was a very busy year for the French military as they were engaged in multiple fronts during the Flanders Campaign with seemingly little gains at first; however, they ultimately ended up winning all of them, including one with the superior British navy during the conflict known as the Glorious First of June. This is usually seen as a big win for France because they had never posed much of a challenge to Britain's navy before since they had the strongest naval fleet in Europe. Despite the success, it came at a high cost as the French Navy lost a quarter of its numbers, but it was still incredibly impressive that they even managed to defeat the British navy at all. Belgium also served as a war venue with the Austrians invading Landrecies and making their way deeper into French territory, creating a constant game of tug-of-war between the French and Austrian armies for the rest of the year. Jean-Baptiste Jourdan led a French auxiliary force on the German border while Jean-Charles Pichegru and Jean Victor Marie Moreau led the main French force in Flanders. By the middle of the year, the French forces had driven out the combined allied forces comprising of the Dutch, the British, and the Austrians, occupying the Rhine territory successfully. Even though the victories of the mainland forces were significant, the performance of the French Navy was not as solid, although it did achieve multiple short-lived victories including the retaking of Martinique by Jean-Baptiste Victor Hugues as well as the Glorious First of June. Nevertheless, the tables had turned against the anti-French coalition as the French Army made its way toward conquering the Dutch Republic the following year.

In 1795, the French Army had made its way to the Dutch Republic, attacking it at the beginning of the year. This was a huge success for the French, mostly because of the Dutch populace joining with the French to start the Batavian Revolution. The Dutch navy was taken over effortlessly, making things immensely difficult for Prussia, which was now on the defensive instead of the offensive after the Dutch practically handed over their navy to the French Army. The Prussians were also trying to occupy Poland, which made it difficult for them to keep fighting on two fronts. On April 6th, 1795, the Prussians signed a peace treaty with the French known as the Peace of Basel which relegated the areas west of the Rhine River as French territory. The French occupation of Catalonia also paid off in 1795 when the Spanish called for peace as well.

The British suffered the most defeats during this year of the French Revolutionary Wars. First of all, they failed in their attempt to support the rebels in Vendee, as they failed to land their troops at Quiberon. Secondly, they attempted to bring down the rebel government of France through espionage tactics, which failed miserably. It's also a good time to mention that France went through constitutional changes during this period as well, leading to the formation of the short-lived and ineffective Directory after the approval of the Constitution of the Year III by the National Convention on August 22nd, 1795. It was a mess because though it had appeared to be a democratic system at first to the public, the election system was not rooted in democracy and was very biased, contributing to the mistrust and inefficiency that led to its fall during Napoleon's coup and the events of 18 Brumaire.

The only major setback for the French during this year was the betrayal of General Jean-Charles Pichegru on the Rhine frontier, which resulted in the forced evacuation of Mannheim, which is located in the modern-day nation of Germany. Pichegru was won over by the Royalists, and this betrayal was part of a larger plan to reinstate the monarchy by crowning the exiled Louis XVIII. However, the French were successful on the other fronts, and the multiple peace treaties signed by the nations that were once a part of the anti-French coalition allowed the French Army passage to nearly everywhere in Europe, making way for some major French incursions in 1796.

1796 is an important year in the French Revolutionary Wars. For the first time since the wars started, the newly formed French Republic was on the offensive instead of being on the defensive. Napoleon, who had already proven himself as a master in the art of war, joined with Jean-Baptiste Jourdan and Jean Victor Marie Moreau in a triple-frontier military campaign. The young commander was assigned to the Italian front while the latter two were assigned to the Rhine front. The results were a mixed bag. Napoleon succeeded in taking over Italy in a daring invasion, taking charge of the poorly equipped Italian military in a speedy manner before implementing his tactics to attack the Italian town of Ceva, which was a major enemy outpost over the Apennines. The veteran commanders Jourdan and Moreau, on the other hand, saw some initial victories in the Rhine campaign by invading Vienna and Bavaria, respectively, before being forced to retreat by Archduke Charles, Duke of Teschen. Of the few equals Napoleon encountered during his lifetime, Archduke Charles was one of them, and as a military figure, he was highly revered in European military circles in his own right. He also fought the French in the Second Coalition Wars, making him one of France's most distinguished opponents during the French Revolutionary Wars.

Napoleon was very busy during the year of 1796. Besides directing his Italian campaign, he was also responsible for the French victory in the Montenotte Campaign. On April 10th, 1796, Johann Peter Beaulieu's Austrian forces launched a surprise attack near Genoa, taking the French Army by surprise. Instead of going on the defensive, Napoleon decided to attack, and he crushed the right wing of the Austrian forces two days later, establishing him as a major figure to contend with. His next major victories in this campaign were the Battle of Millesimo and the Second Battle of Dego before finishing it off with the decisive Battle of Mondovì. This led to the surrender of the Sardinian forces and paved the way for an invasion of the Italian Peninsula, thanks to the newly acquired military locations of Nice and Savoy.

Napoleon's next destination was Italy, which he conquered with relative ease. After the Battle of Mondovì, it was one straight victory after another, thanks to Napoleon's brilliant execution of his ingenious tactics and strategies that baffled his opponents and took them completely by surprise. After the Battle of Fombio and the Battle of Borghetto, by June, Italy was pretty much secured by the French forces. In July and August, the Austrian army tried to mount a counterattack by replenishing the Italian army under the command of Dagobert Sigismund, Count von Wurmser. The French Army broke through their ranks easily in the ensuing battles, cornering the Austrian army completely and defeating them on this front by November of that year. The rebels of Vendee also yielded to a French force led by Louis Lazare Hoche shortly after the Austrian defeat. As part of Napoleon's strategy to cut off the Austrian army from supplies, the Siege of Mantua was started to completely eliminate the Austrian opposition, which came to an end a year later. It was originally snatched from the Austrians earlier during the Italian campaign, but it was here that the Austrian army made their final stand.

By 1797, all of Europe was at war with each other, leaving the French military with some time to breathe. This all-out war also led to the fallout of the anti-French coalition. The Spanish fleet, which had been the enemy of France a few years earlier, changed stances and joined with the French to defeat the British. The British fleet, however, lived up to their legacy and completely defeated the Spanish fleet near Portugal at the Battle of Cape St. Vincent on February 14th. This was not a battle well suited for France, as they had problems competing with the naval forces of some of the other major European powers before the French Revolution even took place. So, instead of taking part in the naval conflict and emboldened by the weakened state of the British navy, the French sent an invasion force to Wales under an experienced Irish-American commander named Captain William Tate. This wasn't a fully-fledged invasion since it was basically a small army of 1,400, which was dubbed *La Legion Noire* (the Black Legion), since Wales was considered to be of little strategic importance. But the fierce local resistance, combined with the ingenuity of renowned naval commander John Campbell, pushed the French back, and Tate was forced into an unconditional surrender on February 24th, two days after they had landed.

However, this was a small loss in the overall war as Napoleon was racking victory after victory in Italy, forcing the Vatican to intercede and declare a peace treaty when the French defeated Count von

Wurmser at the Battle of Rivoli on February 2nd, 1797, after the year-long siege of Mantua which had started the year before. Austria was now open for a direct invasion, and Napoleon wasted no time in marching over the Julian Alps to the center of Austria and sent General Barthélemy Joubert to invade the territory of Tyrol, a separated part of the Austrian kingdom. Archduke Charles of Austria faced his final defeat on March 16th, 1797, at Tagliamento, effectively ending the War of the First Coalition after the Peace of Leoben was signed on April 18th later that year. Austria ceded a number of territories to the French later that year in the Treaty of Campo Formio.

In 1798, after having shown that he was a formidable opponent in the war effort to keep France together, Napoleon turned his attention to Egypt to disrupt Britain's trade with its Indian colonies to weaken the country's economy since he considered the British navy to no longer pose a direct threat due to being weakened in the previous two years of the war, a decision which Napoleon and the French Army came to regret later on. The blame mainly lay on the French Directory who had already started to become jealous of his rising fame and who was scared that keeping him close to the capital of Paris would lead to a possible coup and the rise of a new dictator, overthrowing the delicate power balance achieved through the French Revolution. Despite their efforts in banishing Napoleon in the name of a military campaign, their predictions and fears about Napoleon's influence and rise to power through a coup came to pass eventually.

Staring his voyage from Toulon, France, Napoleon took over Malta while making his way to his final destination of Alexandria. He landed there in June, and he marched to Cairo next, achieving what he had set out for: conquering Egypt through the grand Battle of the Pyramids. But the tables turned shortly after as Admiral Horatio Nelson sunk almost all of Napoleon's fleet at the Battle of the Nile, effectively stranding the military hero of France on the shores of Egypt for about a year.

This was not the only British naval victory over the French in 1798. In the summer, the French sent a fleet of ships and a small military force to assist the Irish rebels in County Mayo, both of which were soundly defeated after some successes. There were also the short-lived sea battles with the newly formed United States of America, known as the "Quasi-War," which was resolved through the Convention of 1800 before it got out of hand and turned into a full-blown war.

While Napoleon spent the better part of 1798 in managing the conquered territories of Egypt, the rest of the French military was occupied on multiple battlefronts in Europe. Taking advantage of the civil strife in Switzerland, the French Army seceded Geneva, forming the short-lived Helvetic Republic. To top it all off, Napoleon deposed Pope Pius VI and formed what the French called the Roman Republic, which was also short-lived. There was also the Peasants' War that occurred during this year, which took place in Luxembourg and the Southern Netherlands, territories the French had acquired in conflicts back in 1794 but were not officially French territories until 1797 due to a treaty signed with Austria. This revolt was short-lived as the rebellion was put down within a short period of under two months.

The War of the Second Coalition

Though the ferocity of the French Army and Napoleon's superb tactics during the War of the First Coalition struck fear in the hearts of the enemies of France, the conflict between France and Britain was far from over. One side possessed superb infantry and cavalry while the other possessed arguably the best naval forces of that time period, balancing out the scales despite the disparity in the geographical sizes of the countries in question. Despite the total defeat at the hand of the French military in 1797, the British victories in 1798 and the stranding of Napoleon, the mastermind behind the numerous major victories of the French Army in the last years of the War of the First Coalition, emboldened the Austrians to form a second, more effective coalition with the British and the Russians, signaling another period of extended warfare, although it was shorter than the War of the First Coalition.

While some of the greatest heroes in French military history were busy spinning the wheels of war to protect the French Republic, the internal affairs of the nation weren't going too well, which became apparent when the leaders of the French Republic effectively banished Napoleon to a different continent in 1798 in the same way the Roman Senate did to Julius Caesar centuries earlier. The Directory, which was the temporary French government between 1795 to 1799, had a hard time taking control of chaotic France. Though their prime objective was the suppression of the Jacobin forces and supporters in the government (which they did achieve, bringing an end to the Reign of Terror), France was still fraught by economic and civil problems which made their work difficult and problematic to no end. Though the reign of the monarchy had been brought down, the corruption and centuries of social disparity were far from over, preventing a united and strong France from being formed.

This made things more complicated as the military might of the new anti-French coalition was much superior than that of the former coalition. Once the newly formed coalition was officially announced, the French Army of Observation, the homeland reserve of the French military who hadn't participated in Napoleon's campaign in Egypt, sprang into action in March 1799 under the banner of Jean-Baptiste Jourdan. Consisting of a total of 30,000 men who were split into four divisions, the army changed its name to the Army of Danube, forsaking its former name after crossing the Rhine. Their final objective was near the Lech River, which was where Archduke Charles had garrisoned his whole army. Spies and emissaries of the Army of the Danube reported the location of the Austrian force to Jourdan, and he decided to forge ahead, confident of France's military might, which ultimately courted disaster. In their first skirmish with the Archduke of Austria, the Army of the Danube suffered serious losses, being forced to retreat first to Messkirch and then to Stockach and Engen. France's second defeat at the Battle of Stockach forced Jourdan to set off for Paris to request more troops and supplies, leaving the command to Jean Augustin Ernouf, his Chief of Staff. Ultimately, Jourdan retired from his command under a medical leave, forcing the recently defeated French Army to reorganize itself.

While all of this was taking place in the European theater of the war, Napoleon was carving his own path to glory through the African theater where he was stranded due to the British navy effectively preventing him from leaving by creating a blockade. With no way to return home, Napoleon started a string of conquests beginning with Syria since the British forces had allied themselves with them, probably hoping to entice Napoleon in a land battle. The first few victories of Napoleon's Syrian campaigns came in the conquests of Jaffa and El Arish, but at the siege of Acre during March 1799, Napoleon finally met his match. Despite months of siege warfare and repeated assaults, all of Napoleon's efforts proved to be naught as his forces were slowly decimated by the combined Syrian and British forces, commanded under Jezzar Pasha and Sir Sydney Smith. Within two months, the same problems that were hampering the Army of the Danube's progress started affecting Napoleon's campaign as well. The Turkish took advantage of the weakened state of Napoleon's forces and spearheaded an assault on Egypt, with the help of the British naval blockade, from Rhodes. However, Egypt was now Napoleon's turf, and he was no longer a foreigner to the desert landscape. He scored a decisive victory over the Turkish at the Battle of Abukir in July, despite his army being undersupplied and affected by a widespread plague that had broken out. It was during this time that news of the military and political strife at home reached Napoleon's ears, prompting him to return home. Leaving his army behind, Napoleon managed to break through the British blockade, determined to take matters into his own hands and stage a coup once he reached Paris, which he did on November 9th.

When Napoleon decided to return home, he also decided to leave the command of the remainder of his forces in Egypt under General Jean-Baptiste Kléber, who had accompanied him on the campaign. Meanwhile, back in Europe, the French Army was desperately trying to keep things together. The remainder of the Army of the Danube after the first incursion against the Archduke of Austria merged with newly formed Army of Helvetia, under the command of André Masséna, one of Napoleon's most dedicated disciples who later became a Marshal of the Empire. After being restructured, the army, consisting of 40,000 men, took part in a series of small battles in the Swiss Plateau region, the Battle of Winterthur on May 27th, 1799, being the chief among them. This was followed by the First Battle of Zurich a few days later, signaling the first loss in the new campaign. Though forced back to Limmat at first by the combined Austrian and Russian army, the French military gained the upper hand once Archduke Charles was ordered to move north across the Rhine River, leaving a force of 25,000 Russian soldiers as well as another 15,000 of his own, under the capable veteran General Friedrich Freiherr von Hotze behind. Although Hotze was capable, the French Army had an easy victory thanks to the poor defensive Russian formations caused by the inexperienced Alexander Korsakov. The French Army successfully occupied northern Switzerland, and the Austrian army was dealt a severe blow at Hotze's death during the Second Battle of Zurich.

In 1800, Napoleon joined up with the Army of the Reserve. The first military action to take place in 1800 was by the defeated Austrian army making a comeback with a two-pronged attack, along with the British, against Masséna's forces. The British navy held a strong naval blockade, denying supplies and naval support to Masséna's forces, while General Michael von Melas of the Austrian army besieged Masséna's forces by land at Genoa with an overwhelming force of 100,000 men, which was vastly superior to Masséna's forces in terms of numbers. This turned out to be one of the most strenuous military sieges in history and one that led to some of Napoleon's biggest military successes in 1800, albeit at the risk of losing Masséna's entire force.

While Masséna was ordered to hold off the siege until June 4th, Napoleon ordered the Army of the Reserve to flank the Austrian army from the rear and provide support to Masséna by crossing the Alps with considerable artillery power and an additional 40,000 troops which he himself led. Though the army crossed the Alps, two major incidents slowed down their progress. For one, a good chunk of the artillery equipment, which had to be painstakingly hauled over the mountains, was prevented in reaching its destination for a few weeks due to an Austrian fort on the Italian side of the Alps. Secondly, a stubborn regiment of 400 Austrian-Piedmontese soldiers dug in their heels against the advancing army. They held out against the huge French Army of 40,000, holding them off for 2 weeks, resulting in the French forces who were crossing the Alps to be delayed by 2 weeks as well. Napoleon barely had time to spare to rush to Masséna's aid as it was now the beginning of June.

However, instead of doing as he planned, Napoleon advanced to take over Milan, hoping to cut off Melas' communication hub to weaken and withdraw his siege of Genoa. Of the few military mistakes Napoleon had made in his life, this was one of them. Not only did General Melas not lift his siege of Genoa, forcing Masséna to give into his terms, but Melas had also prepared for Napoleon's advance. Once Napoleon realized the tactical folly of taking over Milan instead of attacking General Melas' flank, he rushed to Alessandria where Melas' forces were stationed supposedly doing nothing. Again, making an egotistical assumption that his enemy was fleeing, Napoleon dispersed his forces to cut off Melas' escape route. At this point, the Austrians started attacking the broken-up French Army in an organized manner which resulted in the Battle of Marengo on June 14th. Napoleon's forces were on the brink of defeat, but they were saved at the last moment by a counterattack led by an extra detachment of French troops under the command of Louis Desaix, a veteran of the War of the First Coalition who was a recognized war hero from humble origins. Although the battle was won, it came at the price of Desaix's life. This unexpected and stunning victory had General Melas enter into negotiations in which the Austrians ceased military activities in Italy. Leaving the consolidation of the post-war-efforts and a renewed campaign toward Austria to future Marshal of the Empire Guillaume Brune, Napoleon left for Paris to assert his political influence.

All the conflicts throughout the rest of the year were mostly carried out in the German territories where the Austrians had gained significant political alliances, bolstering their numbers despite Melas' defeat. Under the banner of Feldzeugmeister (an archaic term for general and equivalent to the position of general in the Hungarian army in the 17th and 18th centuries) Pál Kray, a huge army was assembled with the combined forces of the Electorate of Bavaria, the Duchy of Württemberg, the County of Tyrol, and the Archbishopric of Mainz, bringing it to a total of 150,000 men. Despite the large manpower gathered, Kray displayed poor tactical choices in setting up his base of operations and spreading out the formation of his army across the Rhine.

His opponent in these German skirmishes was Moreau, who already had his hands full with an ill-equipped and smaller force (130,000), although he was a veteran with about a decade's worth of fighting experience. Napoleon extended a helping hand from Paris by sending him an excellent plan to mount an attack from the Swiss front, but Moreau decided to take glory by using his own talent. Applying a set of complicated maneuvers, Moreau fought against Kray at both Engen and Stockach on May 3rd, resulting in a stalemate with extensive losses on both sides. The French managed to take advantage of Kray's weak positioning of his base of operations, capturing it under General Claude Lecourbe. This maneuver forced Kray to retreat back to Messkirch, and from there, the French Army ultimately forced him to go back as far as Munich after the Battle of Höchstädt and Ulm in the following September and October, respectively. The Austrians held on for a few more months, but they ultimately gave in and signed the Treaty of Lunéville on February 9th, 1801, effectively ending the war for all parties except for Britain and France, who continued their naval skirmishes. Admiral Nelson was particularly fierce in his attacks during this period, attacking French ships and France's allies indiscriminately. The most notable naval skirmishes of 1801 included the First Battle of Algeciras (a French victory) and the Second Battle of Algeciras (a British victory). The British were successful when it came to the land campaign of Egypt as well. Along with the Ottoman forces, they defeated the French at the Battle of Alexandria on March 21st, 1801. Kléber had already been assassinated by this point, being stabbed in June of 1800, and the command had passed to General Jacques-François de Menou. However, despite Menou giving in to the British terms, the hostilities between the French and the Ottoman Empire didn't officially cease until the Treaty of Paris in 1802.

In 1802, the Treaty of Amiens was also signed between France and Britain, supposedly signaling the end of the war, but all it did was act as an interim period of peace until the start of the Napoleonic Wars.

Chapter 3 – The Political Rise of Napoleon Bonaparte

As stated at the end of the last chapter, the peace treaty of 1802 was a short-lived one, signaling another era of conflict between the French and the British over the dominance of Europe. The French Revolutionary Wars had drained the military and civil resources of almost all the major countries in Europe, and the only players left on the board capable of fighting were the French and the British. But to understand the Napoleonic Wars, one must have an understanding of Napoleon Bonaparte himself, which will help to explain many of his actions and decisions throughout his life.

Like many of the heroes of the post-French Revolution era, Napoleon made his way from humble origins to the pinnacle of power, eventually becoming the Emperor of France. The second son (third if counting the infantile death of his sibling) of a minor nobleman in the far-flung island of Corsica, located far away from the French mainland, Napoleon was groomed for a military career since his childhood, as was the custom at that time among noble families. He was born to Carlo Maria di Buonaparte and Maria Letizia Ramolino in 1769, and his original name was Napoleone di Buonaparte. He changed his name to Napoleon Bonaparte when he married at the age of 27 in 1796. Like many other headstrong figures throughout history, Napoleon attributed much of his success in his later life to his mother, who raised the boy with the utmost care and discipline. The typical Corsican family didn't have access to much education and influential positions at that time, as France had bought the rights to it from Genoa the same year Napoleon was born (although it wasn't officially a French province until 1770), but he was lucky enough to have access to better education thanks to his family lineage. In 1779, he was sent to be enrolled in a military school at Brienne-le-Château. There, he learned French along with other subjects; he was particularly good at mathematics. Despite learning French from an early age, Napoleon always had a Corsican accent and never learned to spell properly. He was constantly bullied at school, making him a withdrawn child who solely focused on his studies. After finishing his courses in 1784, he was one of the brilliant few admitted to the École Militaire in Paris, where he trained to become an artillery officer.

Many would think that joining the military was the starting point in Napoleon's political career, but his political reasoning and motivations reached even further back. During the last years of Corsican freedom before it became a province of France, his family was marked as political untouchables and anti-patriotic by Pasquale Paoli, one of Corsica's leading anti-French politicians, prompting Napoleon and his family to emigrate to France as refugees, which is where he had started his aforementioned schooling. Despite being exiled from his homeland, he remained a hard and fast Corsican nationalist throughout his youth, dreaming of a unified Corsica free from French rule. Besides doing his regular studies, Napoleon also studied Corsican and Italian, both major languages of the island. His treatment by his peers at Brienne-le-Châteaualso added to his resentment of the French as he was constantly harassed due to his accent, his short stature, and his Corsican lineage. The same also happened, albeit to a lesser degree, at the École Militaire. So, when the French Revolution broke out in 1789, he saw it as a golden opportunity for a liberated Corsica with him leading the revolutionary charge of a Corsican nationalist movement, despite the bitter exile his family had to face at the hands of Pasquale Paoli.

Napoleon had already finished his studies by this point, and he was stationed at Corsica for two years, from 1789 to 1791, where he attempted to create a good relationship with his countrymen by birth. But what happened next was a bitter experience for Napoleon and one that shaped his military and political ideologies for years to come. To his utter surprise, the Corsican nationalists refused to embrace the revolutionary ideas of equality and liberty that stirred up the rest of the French nation. Perhaps the defamation of his family was still in the minds of the Corsican nationalist leaders, who most likely considered Napoleon to be a French interloper who might have come to sabotage their movement. This frustrated the future Emperor of France so badly that he abandoned his youthful ideals and dedicated himself at last to the role of gaining military glory in France, forsaking his Corsican roots and ties and returning to France in 1791. The bitter cynicism gnawed at him, and he once wrote, "Among so many conflicting ideas and so many different perspectives, the honest man is confused and distressed and the skeptic becomes wicked...Since one must take sides, one might as well choose the side that is victorious, the side which devastates, loots, and burns. Considering the alternative, it is better to eat than to be eaten" about the state of politics after his return to France in 1793. However, this served as his initial training for his trials in the future yet to come, which were both political and military in nature.

As an outsider who had to seek refuge in France to survive, the appeal of the French Revolution was different to the young Napoleon Bonaparte than that of his compatriots, for example, Jourdan, who was a staunch French patriot. The violence and riots on the streets actually angered Napoleon. Indeed, in a letter to his brother Joseph, he mentioned his opinion of the "common people" and wrote two sentences that demonstrate his political beliefs: "When you get right down to it, the crowd is hardly worth the great effort one takes to curry its favor. If Louis XVI had climbed on a horse, victory would have been his."

So, what attracted Napoleon, an ingenious, self-made outsider, to the Revolution? In short, it was the recognition of achievements, both big and small. Napoleon was a Corsican, considered to be an outsider to the mainland French, just like the Algerians who were also French by identity. The Revolution rejected this notion and placed all Frenchmen on an equal pedestal, whether he be a noble or a beggar. That person could be an intellectual or a military officer; it didn't matter as long as it revolved around freedom or liberty.

Later on, Napoleon became a Jacobin, the very same group that was pushing France toward a violent and militaristic regime under the influence of Maximilien Robespierre to whom Napoleon was introduced to by Augustin Robespierre, Maximilien's younger brother, after the Siege of Toulon in July of 1793. The Jacobins were left-wing extremists who grew in power during the early years of the French Revolution, especially after Louis XVI was uprooted from his seat of power in August of 1792. The Reign of Terror, which is historically notorious, was not an act of aggression toward the old elitist society as some historians have claimed, despite the tens of thousands of deaths that occurred. Rather it was the result of attempts to put down counterrevolutionary conspiracies primarily headed by Compte d'Artois and assisted by the former king and queen before they were deposed. The Jacobin regime of the French Revolution also started spinning the wheels of war that would continue to spin until the end of the Napoleonic Wars due to the simple fact that the Jacobins declared their revolutionary principles to be established wherever the French Army was present, effectively declaring a single-handed war against Europe.

The French Revolution and the wars that followed were highly dependent on the brave soldiers of France to ensure the Republic's continued existence against the combined military might of its neighbors. Being an outsider no longer posed a problem to rise through the ranks, especially for military officers like Napoleon, who had the brains and political savviness to see things through. It should be noted that Napoleon was a very pragmatic and practical man, the kind of man some would call an opportunist, but that is exactly what enabled him to reach the highest pinnacle of power in France and change the course of European history forever. He always looked out for himself, and during his early military career, before he had any successful military victories under his belt, he always tried to gain the favor of his superiors.

Napoleon's first major call to action was during the Siege of Toulon in 1793. The British had occupied the small and peaceful Mediterranean town, and Napoleon was put in charge of the French artillery backed by local aristocrat Antoine Christophe Saliceti, as well as Augustin Robespierre. This was the first battle where Napoleon demonstrated his lifelong preference for the tactic of singling out his enemy's weakest point and attacking it to defeat the enemy. Though Napoleon wasn't in charge of the overall siege, his strategic setup of the artillery batteries that supported the troops by raining down bombardment over Fort de l'Éguillette (the Needle) turned out to be the winning factor of the siege, forcing the British to evacuate the port city within hours of the French laying siege on Toulon. Napoleon was promoted to Brigadier General soon after his accomplishments reached Paris via Augustin Robespierre's letter to his elder brother.

Napoleon's acquaintance with the Jacobin leaders actually might have cut his career short, but fortunately, he was acquitted of any wrongdoing. In 1794, a group known as the Thermidorians had had enough of the extremist policies that were being implemented and used by the Robespierre-led Jacobin faction. They executed them both along with some of their supporters, and they blacklisted all of their known supporters and acquaintances. Though the Jacobins had led the charge of the Revolution and drew the attention of the masses to direct their anger at culling the elites of the former monarchist France to retain their positions after putting down the flames of the old monarchy, they did little to nothing to improve the internal economic and civil conditions of the country, which had been in very bad shape to begin with without the costly war campaigns tacked on. When the common populace realized this, the Jacobins lost their main tool of power and were swiftly routed. The Thermidorians mainly consisted of the middle-class French citizens who were now the new aristocrats of France, amassing their wealth and connections during the Revolution. Since the anger of the poor people were now slowly starting to divert toward them, as they were effectively the new nobility in France, they swiftly took action against the Jacobins, who, fortunately for the Thermidorians, had already started losing the support of the people. After the Jacobins were deposed, the Thermidorians took over a majority in the National Convention.

Napoleon found himself under house arrest for his known connections with the Robespierres, and he might have suffered a similar fate under the guillotine had it not been for his military genius and his formal letter of defense through which he tactfully secluded himself from the Jacobin circles. The necessity of the new Thermidorian reactionaries had a part to play in Napoleon's release as well, as many of the former Royalists saw this as a chance to put the monarchy back in order. Civil unrest erupted all over the country, centering on the issue of the impoverished economy, and in October 1795, the new Directory was besieged by counterrevolutionary Royalists determined to put an end to the Revolutionary regime. General Paul Barras was called to quell down the rebellion, and Napoleon Bonaparte, who was now a subordinate of Barras, led the charge. Gunning down innocent civilians was no mean feat, but Napoleon saw it through by ordering cannon fire on the approaching mob, calling it a "whiff of grapeshot." Once the smoke had cleared, over 200 lay dead on the streets by official count. This was the unofficial beginning of Bonapartism, which Napoleon maintained throughout his rule. The basis of this ruling system was a strong and authoritative military which would maintain control of the state instead of civilians by placing the needs of the state (effectively meaning the army) over the common populace. This idea of ruling allowed the Napoleonic Wars to be waged effectively once Napoleon took power. After this incident, a new constitution was created which got rid of the National Convention and created a new one instead, known as the Directory. This was a five-member committee that governed France between November 2nd, 1795, and November 9th, 1799, when it was overthrown by Napoleon.

The new Thermidorian-led France was as bad, if not worse, than the elitist society preceding the French Revolution. While the Reign of Terror had scared many of the wealthy into hiding their fortunes, they started to show their wealth again after the Jacobins were uprooted. But to do this, they needed the public eye to rest on something else or, in this case, someone else. Napoleon's suppression of the October revolt made him somewhat of a celebrity in Parisian circles, and for the first time in his career, he started amassing political power as much as military recognition. The Thermidorians sealed their fate once Barras promoted Napoleon to the position of Chief of Police; this was the most powerful position in the Directory, effectively making him the most powerful person in France when it came to internal affairs of the country. And he had achieved all of this by the age of 26. Threatened by his growth from zero to hero, some members of the Directory conspired to send him out of the country under the pretense of the Italian and Egyptian campaigns of the War of the Second Coalition, which ultimately proved to be ineffective in the long run.

But before his campaign in Egypt took place, the newly minted hero had much to prove in the war theatres on his home front. As mentioned earlier, the War of the Second Coalition was already in full swing by this time, and the Austrian army had occupied Italy to launch its attack on France. Lazare Carnot, the man who introduced the idea of levée en masse (universal conscription) aided Napoleon greatly during this time by encouraging the conscripted poor and ill-fed masses as a means to have food in their bellies and clothes on their backs. This allowed the poorly equipped French Army led by Napoleon to gain victory over the superiorly equipped Austrian army again and again in multiple skirmishes, defeating the Habsburgs and gaining control of the Austrian Netherlands in the process.

It was during this time that Napoleon consolidated absolute military power and gained the unquestionable loyalty of his men. Before setting out for the Italian campaign, he gave a rousing speech to the French troops which went along like this: "Soldiers, you are ill-fed and almost naked [...] I shall lead you into the most fertile plains of the world, where you will find big cities and rich lands. You will gather honor, glory and riches." He kept true to his word but at the expense of the newly conquered Italian territories and the betrayal of the very Italians who welcomed the French Army with open arms when they drove off the Austrians. The French Army plundered and looted the Italian peasants to their heart's content, since for the first time since their conscription, they were actually getting paid and rewarded for putting their lives on the line for the sake of their motherland.

Unlike many military figures of his time whose sole focus was on glory, his time at Parisian balls and meetings had made Napoleon a shrewd and cunning politician as well. During the Italian campaign, he established two newspapers called the *Courrier de l'Armée d'Italie* and *La France vue de l'Armée d'Italie* to serve as propaganda machines, with one being circulated for the troops in his army and the other being circulated in France. Each of his victories was loudly declared through these newspapers, increasing his popularity and decreasing that of the Directory. So, despite being far from home, Napoleon was able to amass popularity and political power. There was another good reason for the Directory to be afraid of Napoleon as well; without express permission from the Directory, Napoleon had engaged in negotiations with the pope as well as the King of Naples.

Tired of his bravado and increasing popularity, the Directory sent him to the quell the British, who had proven to be the strongest foe for the Republic, after the celebrated general returned from Italy.

Napoleon moved back and forth with his plans, but the one factor that ruined his strategies was the impossibly strong British navy.

So, instead, Napoleon tried the strategy of starting internal dissent in British territories by promising support to the Irish who were fighting to free themselves from British rule instead of direct confrontation with the British navy. However, the insurrection failed due to the efforts of the Royal Navy. Due to the failure of this strategy, Napoleon focused his attack on the British by waging a military campaign in another continent to disrupt British commercial interests. If Napoleon could control the Eastern Mediterranean through Egypt, it would strike a serious blow to British resources who relied on India as a trading partner. The anti-Napoleon segment of the Directory wholeheartedly supported this strategy as a means to keep Napoleon away from the political picture and public attention, even though they knew full well that the wars in the European theater were far from over and that they would be unable to support Napoleon's foreign campaign for an extensive period of time.

It should be noted that Napoleon couldn't help but compare himself to Alexander the Great when he planned to capture Egypt to disrupt Britain's naval power since the legendary general had also done the same thing, crossing an entire continent to dominate another. This inflated ego encouraged Napoleon to take intellectuals like archeologists and scholars with him, another thing that Alexander had done in his campaigns to learn of the new world he was about to conquer. Despite being a decision born out of Napoleon's flamboyant ego, which had started showing since his ascent to military power after the Siege of Toulon, this decision proved useful as his team actually made many modern discoveries throughout their voyage to Egypt, including the discovery of the Rosetta Stone, the key to deciphering Egyptian hieroglyphics.

Napoleon's first Egyptian victory was in Alexandria, one of Egypt's major port cities, which didn't prove to be much of a problem since the Egyptian navy and the city's defenses were easy enough for

Napoleon's army to break through. But after that victory, everything about the Egyptian campaign started falling into shambles.

It should be evident that the topography of Africa, with its vast deserts, is very different from the topography of Europe, which is made of highlands and mountains. As a result, Napoleon's forces were anything but ready for battle as they did not know the first thing about desert warfare. This was practically proven when Napoleon started his attack on Cairo. The glorious siege tactic that had worked so well for Napoleon in his other battles fell flat as his men started dying from thirst and heat, two things the French Army were not accustomed to. The conditions were so bad that many men attempted to commit suicide out of sheer madness. This was an army accustomed to living off the land it occupied, but the desolate desert offered no such solace to Napoleon's army. Despite the dire conditions, the one silver lining that the French Army had was that they had superior military tactics and equipment compared to the Egyptian, Mamluk, and Turkish armies that they had to face. Mamluks were slave warriors belonging to the Turkish army and had a fierce reputation for their cavalry units, which the French were not aware of. The first conflict, which was the Battle of the Pyramids on July 21st, 1798, between Napoleon's forces against the Turks and Mamluks was a decisive victory, but Admiral Nelson, who was Britain's answer to Napoleon, sunk almost his entire fleet at the Battle of the Nile, stranding the proud French commander on the shores of Africa with no way to head home due to the British blockade. So, Napoleon sought the only possible recourse that he could take at that point: march forward. But before that, he spent the better part of a couple of months strengthening his position in Egypt, understanding the topography, and overseeing the administration of the captured territories.

Napoleon fought a series of campaigns in Syria, encountering many victories until he faced his second obstacle in the Egyptian campaign—Acre. Acre was well fortified, and their defenses were under the command of two commanders of great renown, Jezzar

Pasha and Commodore Sydney Smith. After several months of failed attempts to take over the city, Napoleon retreated back to Cairo where the news of the deteriorating conditions of the French homeland and the damage caused by the weak and corrupt Directory reached his ears. He immediately resolved to return home, taking his chance to break through a weak segment of the British blockade.

While it is true that his victories in Egypt were one of the low points of his military career, the fact that he was winning was encouraging to the general populace due to the defeats that they were facing in Europe. Napoleon made his way back to Paris, where he found the situation ripe for a coup. People were tired with the moral and political bankruptcy of the Directory and were desperate for a change, looking for a figure of hope to look up to. Napoleon returned from Egypt not a moment too soon to present himself as the ideal candidate to the French people.

The funny thing is, the Directory actually did send out orders for him to return from Egypt due to the continuous defeats in the European war theater, but Napoleon set out for France before those orders reached him. Once he arrived back in France, he was greeted with a hero's welcome. Napoleon now commanded the loyalty of the military and the common people, aided by the newspapers which touted his victories. To the average French commoner, he was one of them, a nobody who rose to great power by his talent and hard work, not to mention that he was the one further increasing France's territorial holdings. This was, of course, not true at all judging from the fact that this man was dispassionate enough to kill his own countrymen to quell a rebellion, but as the saying goes, stories tend to become truer than the truth itself, and this is exactly what happened in Napoleon's case.

Napoleon made an alliance with Emmanuel Joseph Sieyès, his brother Lucien, Joseph Fouché, and Charles-Maurice de Talleyrand. Together, they planned a coup to overthrow the Directory. It was a total success, thanks to Napoleon's public popularity as well as public dissatisfaction to how things were running under the new government. His main accomplice in the Coup of 18 Brumaire (Brumaire was the second month in the French Republican calendar) was Emmanuel Joseph Sieyès, a key French Revolutionary figure who bore much dislike toward the Directory and who had public popularity as well. Initially, he thought he was using Napoleon by letting him get his hands dirty then seize political power after the dust had cleared; however, it was actually the other way around. Napoleon used him to lead the Coup of 18 Brumaire and then became the most powerful man in France.

Napoleon's rise to the position of First Consul after the coup was not as glorious as his military victories. Though a hardened and elegant inspirer of men, his public-speaking skills were anything but passable, and when he appeared before the Thermidorian Convention formed shortly after overthrowing the Robespierre brothers to state his case, he was booed and jeered by opponents from all sides. Only the fear of his loyal army forced the members to appoint him as the First Consul. This was done through the new constitution, known as the Constitution of the Year VIII. With this move, Napoleon effectively became a dictator because although the constitution assigned executive power to three consuls, only the First Consul held any real power. In allowing a vote to pass this constitution in February of 1800, Napoleon was able to maintain an appearance of democracy, although it wouldn't have mattered either way because the vote was not binding.

Though Napoleon had assembled his political power through unscrupulous means, he was by no means ignorant of the conditions of France and the events that led to his rise to power. He was plagued with a crumbling economy, civil unrest, and a demoralized French population who hung their heads in shame due to the recent losses in Europe. Napoleon had a lot on his plate when he sat down on the throne of power, and it took him two years to stabilize the nation and the war fronts France was engaged in to start the Napoleonic Wars against the British to become the one and only superpower in Europe.

Chapter 4 – The Rise of Bonapartism: An Alternative Monarchy Readying for the Napoleonic Wars

The rise of Napoleon was effectively the end of the French Revolution. Instead of a group of squabbling politicians and intellectual and military leaders who couldn't agree on anything productive and were internally distrustful of each other, the French masses had finally found a leader who could lead them. Napoleon had proven this to the peasants by providing them with new land from his conquests as well as being their military leader while the business class benefited from the constant stream of requisitions which boomed their businesses and filled their pockets. The only class whose heart Napoleon couldn't truly win were the plebeians, the working class who made up the core of former Jacobin supporters in the government. So, when he rose to power as First Consul, he made promises to both the left-wing, which was comprised of ex-Jacobins who wished to reinstate the rule they had in the early years of the Revolution, and the right-wing, which was comprised of ex-Royalists of the Directory, to appease them both, but he didn't keep them in the end. What Napoleon did instead was combine the best of both worlds and create an imperial system that took advantage of the functionalities of both ruling types.

Napoleon couldn't have accomplished this very easily, but multiple conspiracies and assassination attempts from both the Royalist and Jacobin factions made things easier for him, giving him the perfect excuse to enforce the imperial system. He did this by establishing a secret police headed by his trusted aid Fouché, who became the chief of the secret police. Napoleon was very adamant about securing his newfound power and uprooted every last person or object related with the Revolution to ensure no further interim unrest disturbed his regime, as his was one built on conquest and military dominance, something that required him to leave his base of power frequently. The most notable of the many attempts to dethrone Napoleon were the Conspiracy of Daggers, which is considered by many historians to be a plot set up by Napoleon's police to discredit the Jacobins, and the Plot of the Rue Saint-Nicaise, where explosives were used in between a narrow pass in the hopes of crushing a carriage that Napoleon was traveling in on a journey to the opera with boulders from the resulting explosion.

The new imperial system called the Consulate, which was created by the First Consul after the events of the 18th Brumaire, contained all the traces of the old regime, such as the nobility and titles, but the aristocratic power that came with these factors were greatly stripped to a bourgeois fashion so as to not slip back to the old monarchist regime again. Even though technically he shared power with other consuls in a seemingly democratic manner, it was more or less an autocratic government system with Napoleon at the top doing what he wanted until he finally declared himself Emperor in 1804. Based on the social model of ancient Rome, the economy flourished better than it had in decades, placating the French commoners. Napoleon created a new constitution in the spring of 1802 that would make the Consulate permanent and Napoleon dictator for life, and 3.6 million came out to vote in a semi-democratic manner, approving the referendum. This was a clever move by the First Consul—he had established himself as the top man of the empire without declaring himself royalty, which the French now hated with heart and soul. In fact, during his time as First Consul, he received a letter from the exiled younger brother of Louis XVI, Louis XVIII, who promised amnesty should the monarchy be restored with Napoleon's aid. The First Consul refused politely, probably with a mischievous smile on his face, replying back to him that the possibility was out of the question.

Some historians say that one of Hitler's main inspirational heroes was Napoleon and that there are striking similarities in their personality and actions. Though Hitler didn't bother with legitimizing his rule with any of the political facades Napoleon had, Hitler's Germany possessed uncanny similarities with Napoleon's France. Both were police states, both had leaders who inspired their people to be superior and militaristic, and both tried to unify and expand their country's borders. One of the facades that Napoleon displayed was in the motto "Equality, Liberty, and Fraternity," which was echoed across a turbulent Europe, causing civil unrest in more than one country. But the truth was that Napoleon formed a police state through the Napoleonic Code which solidified the power base of the middle class. Unlike many dictators in history, he didn't provoke the peasant class as they were an important part of his power base.

On the outside, the Napoleonic Code was the exact embodiment of the ideals he preached—equality, liberty, and fraternity. Under his code, every citizen was deemed equal under the eyes of the law, effectively meaning that everyone was responsible for contributing and developing the state. Everyone had to pay taxes, whether they were a peasant, worker, soldier, or a businessman. To legitimize the presence of the Catholic Church which the French had grown to deride over the course of the French Revolution, he introduced the freedom of religion which ensured that everyone was free to practice religion without the persecution that came with the feudalistic monarchy in which the Church condemned the followers of other religions as heretics. The Napoleonic Code also dealt a crushing blow to the old guilds and unions by providing freedom of profession. This might sound simple, but the impact it had on the socio-economic professional was staggering. Trade and commerce flourished, allowing for a more diversified national economy. T

One of the best things about the Napoleonic Code was that education was no longer an elitist privilege. Napoleon was determined to create an educated nation in order to avoid anything like the French Revolution occurring again. He knew that one of the reasons he was so popular was because he made his way to the top despite being an outsider and coming from more humble origins, and he wanted his people to feel the same way, that they could control their own fate with talent and education. The Napoleonic Code basically legitimized his military dictatorship by introducing an informal constitution for the people that appeared as a benevolent civil code because Napoleon knew no matter how hard he tried to scrub away the stains of the French Revolution, it would always stay in the minds of the people who had wrung power from the monarchy with their own hands. By turning himself into a constitutional monarch, he was effectively proclaiming that his rule was the result of the Revolution. In fact, an important statement of Bonapartism is, "I am the Nation."

However, what the Napoleonic Code secretly did was consolidate the power of the new society of industrialists and businessmen who had gained their wealth from the profitable business of war that was bought by the French Revolutionary Wars, as well as standardize the way peasants could own land. The working class became burdened by this, and it came to the point that they had to carry permits to be shown during random police searches; otherwise, they would be marked as vagabonds and thrown out of the city. In any kind of worker-employer conflict, the employer's word reigned supreme. The censorship of media under the Napoleonic Code was also surprising, considering the fact that it advocated education and free-thinking. During Napoleon's regime, there were less than five newspapers circulating nationwide. One major reason for such strict censorship probably was because most of the newspapers were run by Jacobins and ex-Royalists, so Napoleon didn't want the same power that popularized him to be the source of his downfall as well. In this aspect, Napoleon's paranoia and cynicism is quite clear through the way he dealt with the last remnants of the French Revolution with Fouché and his secret police, using false accusations, assassinations, and other tactics to completely suppress the other side, much the same as Hitler did before and during the Second World War.

It was hard for anyone to go against Napoleon, but it was even harder considering the Church was on his side. During this period, the Church consolidated and legitimized much of Napoleon's authority, which made it difficult for his opponents to build up an effective coalition during the first half of the Napoleonic Wars, as well as during his second invasion of Italy after his rise to power as the First Consul of France. The negotiations that Napoleon had carried out during the first Italian campaign without the authority of the Directory paved the way for the Church to find its foothold into France once again, which was one of the largest and most powerful nations at the time. The lack of a papal hierarchy in France meant a huge loss in revenue since the Church received part of the revenue generated by the people's taxes and was a part of the original Estates General that existed before the pre-Revolution period. Napoleon ensured that when Catholicism was restored back under his rule that he would have the final word in the French clerical hierarchy. The biggest example of his control of the Church included the appointment of bishops from across the nation; in other countries, the bishops were directly appointed from the Vatican. Napoleon understood that though the Revolution had its merits, there was no way the class disparity could be decentralized; he knew that religion would be needed in order to maintain some kind of balance among the people. Despite the benefits this brought, the people in his inner circle were highly displeased that Catholicism had made its way back to the soil of France, as it had been one of the primary targets of the Revolution to abolish religious corruption, and many of his loyal military officers still held a grudge against the establishment. There is a story that Napoleon once asked one of his close military generals how he felt about religious customs while attending a ritual as a customary visit, to which the general boldly replied, "Pretty monkish mummery! The only thing that is missing is the blood of the million men who died trying to overturn what you are restoring."

The casual reader might wonder why the French so readily fell back to the same system they were trying to abolish in the first place. To understand this, one must understand the fundamental nature of a revolution: change. A revolution is a transformative phase that is usually triggered as a result of multiple reasons that drive the masses to call for a change, or it could be the result of an explosion of suppressed fury that can be triggered by a single isolated accident. Either way, the enthusiasm and energy of the outburst lasts for a short time, and any transformation or change a revolution tries to achieve must take place within that time or a revolution is doomed to fail, a common lesson learned from the history of revolutions across multiple cultures, countries, and continents since the beginning of recorded human history. If the change is not achieved, the enthusiasm dies out, and the masses reluctantly accept failure and fall back to their oppressed lifestyle. This was the case of the French Revolution, which is unique in the manner that it succeeded in transforming the feudalistic monarchy society, that had been the custom since the Dark Ages, to the modern democratic society that a good portion of the world enjoys today, ensuring and securing the rights of the common man. However, the people failed to secure a proper revolution due to the indifferences and conflicts between themselves. Although there were events, such as the storming of the Bastille and the Women's March, among others, that caused the initial sparks of the French Revolution to be successful at first, the political conflicts between opposing sides grew, and civil war gripped the nation by the end of the 1790s. The people looked toward Napoleon to guide them, and by placing their trust in him, it made it that much easier for Napoleon to bring firm discipline to the country.

Chapter 5 – The Beginning of the Napoleonic Wars

The enmity and bad blood between the French and the British could be traced back to the Anglo-Saxon times when the English were under the yoke of French rule. Richard the Lionheart, one of the most romanticized English monarchs whose legends and feats parallel King Arthur's, could directly trace his lineage to French origins, but England cut ties with their French cousins later on, creating contention for centuries to come. The rise and supremacy of the British navy was the result of preventing another French invasion. By the time the French Revolutionary Wars started, the British were strong enough to stand toe-to-toe economically and militarily with the European superpowers at the time, Spain, Portugal, and France. The British participation in the War of the Second Coalition affected the outcomes of the skirmishes the French participated in quite negatively, something that Napoleon understood quite well during his first foreign campaign to Egypt where he learned about the supremacy of the Royal Navy the hard way. However, to keep the momentum of his military regime moving forward, Napoleon entered into a second era of wars with the British, who formed different coalitions to thwart the French rule and the threat it brought along with it through the socio-economic shifts that were already taking place within France and its surrounding sister republics, which made it difficult for the British Empire to secure a place of power in continental affairs.

For the first few years of power, Napoleon focused on building his army and, more importantly, his naval forces to match the British whom he knew from firsthand experience would turn out to be his strongest foe when he started his military campaigns. His prior experience in trying to instigate insurrection to destabilize Britain internally had failed, and he lacked the resources to stir any trouble within the British mainland; thus, he opted to face their naval forces head-on. He also consolidated his power and the security of the French Republic under his rule by completely defeating Austria, their major foe who led to the start of the French Revolutionary Wars, in 1800. Napoleon was making Europe his own personal playground and was reorganizing entire countries into an imperial system that were becoming sister republics of France, bearing freedom and individuality in outward appearances only, like Italy and Switzerland.

Napoleon also started impacting the political influence Britain had gained during the War of the Second Coalition, pointing out to European nations that since it was not a part of mainland Europe, it had no role in mainland European politics. He also started meddling with the British trade agreements that were a part of the Treaty of Amiens, which was signed in 1802 and signaled the end of the French Revolutionary Wars. This resulted in the loss of trade for the British, and this action only added fuel to the fire. Combining this with the historical enmity between the two nations, another war was almost inevitable, and in May of 1803, the Napoleonic Wars started, lasting for almost twelve and a half years before finally ending in November of 1815. It had started after the British violated the conditions of the Treaty of Amiens and started a naval blockade against France, which eventually responded with the Continental System.

Until 1805, though, there were no major coalitions to speak of, as both England and France were trying to instigate each other with indirect military action that vested the other party's interest. Napoleon, who became the Emperor of France in 1804, enforced the Continental System, a policy which prohibited British commerce from running through Europe via land, and the British responded back vehemently by placing naval blockades on major French sea-trading routes. Neither the French nor the British had forgotten that they had each tried to separately bring down the other's empire from within, so ultimately, peace was out of the question. Only one of these superpowers could be left standing after the smoke of war had cleared from the European war theater.

Chapter 6 – The Napoleonic Wars, Part 1

Since the backbone of Napoleon's power were the businessmen and industrialists who had made a killing out of almost a decade of war, they were not very keen on maintaining a peaceful state of affairs in Europe. This also aligned well with Napoleon's regime, which was mainly based on vesting the general people's interest in the military efforts and victories to stave off the internal civil problems of the nation, like a corrupt economy or a cunning return to the monarchist state of affairs before the Revolution. The Napoleonic Code, which was enforced throughout the new republic, was also applied in the new sister republics that Napoleon was quietly forming since his rise to the position of First Consul in 1799. Unlike Hitler's direct oppression of conquered countries, which led to direct resentment against the Nazi regime, the Napoleonic code was more tactful in nature. The main aim of the taxation system was so that the army could live off the lands of each nation it conquered and bolster the core of the French economy exponentially.

However, in the same way the masses of France grew disillusioned by the French Revolution, the new sister republics of France were starting to grow tired of Napoleon's oppressive police state and of funding his ever-burgeoning military empire. Napoleon hit the last nerve by enforcing the Continental System, which banned trade with the British in French-controlled territories. This allowed Britain to form more successful coalitions against Napoleon that eventually led to his downfall.

The War of the Third Coalition

Two years after the British had officially declared war against France, it formed the Third Coalition to wage war with Napoleon, mainly due to the rumors that Napoleon was planning an invasion of Britain. Napoleon did consider an invasion of Britain as it was the only country that had been a thorn in his side from his French Revolutionary War campaigns, and so, he amassed a force of 180,000 troops and a very capable artillery unit with the intent to do so. As a result, he started poking and prodding the British navy in the West Indies in the month of July 1805, prompting the British to form the Russian alliance. After entering into agreements with Russia, both sides signed a treaty that enacted an alliance to free the Bavarian Republic (the modern-day Netherlands) and the Swiss Confederation from Napoleon's yoke. With nothing to lose, Austria also joined the Third Coalition, and soon after, Sweden joined the fray, allowing the British to use their country as their base of military operations in August of 1805.

Napoleon's army, which was known as *La Grande Armée* (the Grand Army) for the duration of the Napoleonic Wars, consisted of the troops he had amassed a while back for the invasion of Britain, which numbered to a total of 200,000 infantry units and which grew to 350,000 by the time the skirmishes of the Third Coalition had started, and between 250 and 280 cannons which were divided into 7 corps. Each corps had enough supplies to last a day if entrenched in defensive positions, allowing other corps enough time to come to its rescue. In addition to the infantry division, Napoleon also organized a reserve cavalry division of 22,000 with 24 artillery pieces, for the first time with cuirassiers (cavalry soldiers with muskets) being the main backbone of the reserve. Opposing this hulking military presence was the hardened Russian infantrymen, who were war veterans, and an inexperienced and undertrained Austrian army newly formed in 1801 by Archduke Charles after his previous defeats. The caveat of the Austrian army was its cavalry units, which were still considered the best in Europe at that time despite multiple defeats at the hands of the French in the previous two coalitions.

The Austrians struck the first blow with the invasion of Bavaria with an army of about 70,000 men under Karl Mack von Leiberich. The Austrian army was ill-matched against Napoleon's forces, and the Austrians suffered a significant loss at the Battle of Ulm, though, thankfully, without much loss of life. They also lost a second battle in Italy where Archduke Charles led the charge against Masséna's forces.

The Ulm campaign started it off, which was comprised of five main battles: The Battle of Wertingen, the Battle of Günzburg, the Battle of Haslach-Jungingen, the Battle of Elchingen, and the battle of Ulm. Unlike the previous continental wars Napoleon had waged, which were mainly contained within the Italian Peninsula, Napoleon chose the Danube and the Rhine to be his battle theater, which fooled his enemies into setting up their base of operations in the Italian Peninsula when Napoleon's army was marching through the Danube with one victory after another. This was also the first time he displayed the use of complex battle strategies by using a part of his forces to fool the enemy into thinking that he was taking one route, while in reality, he was flanking the enemy from behind, encircling the enemy forces and making them chase his decoy units. While the Coalition forces faced toward Italy, expecting Napoleon's forces to appear any day, the French Army was encircling Augsburg by marching toward the Black Forest, with the left wing marching from the direction of northern Germany and the Netherlands while the right and center wings moved from the middle of the Rhine.

The invasion of Ulm started on September 22nd along the Iller river. The skirmish went on until the end of September, which was when, after observing the course of the skirmish, Napoleon decided to make Ulm his first objective instead of Augsburg like he originally intended. This was due to General Mack's adamancy at holding the lines at Ulm, which made it easier for Napoleon to change his objective from disrupting Mack's communication lines by taking over Augsburg to obliterating his foe's army with the strategic advantage offered by the topography of the region.

The first conflict in Wertingen on October 8th was a small skirmish between the French forces, led by Marshals Joachim Murat and Jean Lannes, and the Austrian forces, under Lieutenant Field Marshal **Franz Xavier von Auffenburg**. Napoleon's forces had the upper hand since the enemy was totally unaware that Napoleon was coming from behind. The defeated Austrian army made its way back to Ulm two days later.

Michel Ney, one of Napoleon's key military figures and a future Marshal of the Empire, at that time was under the command of Marshal Louis Alexandre Berthier. Ney was ordered to attack Ulm by his commander on October 8th and made his way toward the town of Günzburg, which was on the way to Ulm. This move culminated into the Battle of Günzburg, in which the French forces, led by the General of the 3rd Division, Jean-Pierre Firmin Malher, wrested control of a major crossing across the Danube from Konstantin Ghilian Karl d'Aspré's Austrian forces. This was followed by the battles of Haslach-Jungingen and of Elchingen, ending in the Battle of Ulm which saw the Austrian forces surrendering. After the Battle of Ulm, which lasted from October 16th to October 19th, Napoleon took a break to let his soldiers catch their breath and marched on to occupy Vienna on November 13th. But this proved to be a disadvantageous move since he moved farther away from his army's supply line than he intended. An Austro-Russian joint army, under the command of the Russian military hero and later Field Marshal of the Russian army, Prince Mikhail Illarionovich Golenishchev-Kutuzov, took advantage of Napoleon's distance from his supply lines; Tsar Alexander I of Russia was present at the battle as well. Napoleon's army of 52,000, which was split from the main force to attract the enemy's attention, withstood a siege of nineteen days, and on December 2nd, he achieved a great victory over the Austro-Russian military forces in the Battle of Austerlitz, which is considered to be Napoleon's greatest victory in his career.

One of the main reasons for this victory was Napoleon's psychological maneuvers that made his enemies play right into his hands. While this is definitely true, another reason for the Austro-Russian defeat was due to the Russian and Austrian commanders not being able to agree on anything. Archduke Charles and Kutuzov favored a defensive plan of action, but the Russian tsar, blinded by glory and arrogance, wanted a mounted offensive along with the Austrians. Kutuzov was even unofficially stripped of his command for not agreeing with his monarch to mount a frontal assault against Napoleon's seemingly weaker forces. These forces seemed weaker than usual to those who knew nothing about warfare, but it was noticed by the experienced Kutuzov and Archduke Charles as a decoy strategy.

The two commanders were correct in their assumption. On the eve of the battle, Napoleon had purposefully depopulated his light flank at Pratzen Heights to make the enemy think the ranks were thinned out and that a charge would expose and break through the enemy formation. Napoleon was counting on this to happen, which it did. By charging through his right flank, the Coalition forces exposed their middle and left flanks, which Napoleon's army charged into as soon as the Coalition army fell for Napoleon's trap. The individual corpses of the La Grande Armée, which is what Napoleon's army was called during the Napoleonic Wars, showed their efficiency by bearing down on the enemy flanks from multiple directions, while behind Napoleon lay besieged by the Coalition forces on the frontlines.

The bulk of the battle occurred at Sokolniz, a village that was in a constant state of tug-of-war between the two sides throughout the day since the number of Coalition soldiers charging through the right flank was not high enough in numbers, making it impossible to move to the next phase of Napoleon's plan. It was General Jean-de-Dieu Soult's corps that turned the tide of the battle by breaking through the enemy rear ranks, which they were not expecting. This caused the most casualties on that day due to the element of surprise. While Soult's army was ripping the right flank apart, General Dominique Vandamme's forces were causing havoc on the left flank, approaching through an area called Staré Vinohrady. Even though the left and the right flanks were secured by the French Army, the left flank was attacked again by the Russian Imperial Guardsmen, led by the Russian emperor's brother Grand Duke Constantine, who defeated an entire French battalion in his fierce counterattack, forcing Napoleon to use his cavalry reserve to meet the assault.

With a fierce cavalry battle underway, there was no clear advantage for either side until General Jean-Baptiste Drouet of the 1st Corps flanked the Russian forces from the rear again, like Soult's first assault on the right flank. This move totally devastated the Austro-Russians forces, who became sandwiched between the two French commanders' forces, resulting in another massacre and the loss of lives. The northernmost part of the battlefield also saw fierce fighting under General Kellerman and General Cafarelli, who held their ground after sending Joachim Murat, one of Napoleon's Marshal of the Empire, to lead two of the reserve cuirassier divisions under General Nansuty and General d'Hautpoul to thin down the overwhelming Russian forces. But the final battlefront turned out to be the left flank, which was the village of Sokolnitz during the early part of the day but was now Telinitz, another village close to Sokolnitz. A final double-pronged attack totally ripped apart the coalition forces, sending the enemy into a total retreat and securing French victory.

The French Army suffered a loss of 7,000 men while the opposing army faced a crushing loss of 25,000 men thanks to Napoleon's superior tactics and artillery setup, which was the best at that time at the Battle of Austerlitz. Austria didn't participate in another war against France until the War of the Fifth Coalition. In signing the

Treaty of Pressburg on December, 26th, 1805, Austria agreed to withdraw from the war, and it handed over the Austrian regions of Venetia and the Tyrol to Napoleon's forces.

But despite just winning the greatest military victory in his career, the wars were far from over as the Russians had yet to show their military might, which was numerically the only match for Napoleon's forces in Europe. Thus, the War of the Third Coalition ended by the end of 1805 on an uncomfortable note as trouble was still brewing amongst the anti-French coalition instigated by the British. Napoleon's many victories had his enemies on their toes, and the Battle of Austerlitz had left many of them convinced that agreeing to terms of peace with the mighty nation of France might be the best solution. This was especially true for the Russians, but Napoleon's massive ego would have none of it.

Many historians agree that Napoleon's rule might have lasted much longer and could have been more successful had he decided to consolidate his victories instead of marching forward to gain more of them. He had total control over central Europe, with his kingdom covering Germany, Italy, Belgium, and the Netherlands, all regions with abundant natural resources and manpower that could have turned the wheel of the French empire into a more glorious one. This was also the same mistake Hitler made when he advanced through Europe in his conquests during World War II—both leaders didn't know when to stop and strengthen themselves; instead, they marched forward, thinking only of themselves and of their armies as being invincible forces of nature.

The War of the Fourth Coalition

The War of the Fourth Coalition started shortly after Austria signed the Treaty of Pressburg. As mentioned previously, Napoleon had no intention of stopping his conquest to take over Europe and started forming his own coalition known as the Confederation of the Rhine and started recruiting many of the smaller German states that were a part of his newly conquered kingdom. He elevated the rulers of the

Kingdoms of Saxony and Bavaria, the two largest states in the Confederation, giving them the title of "king.". Saxony was a part of the Fourth Coalition at first but allied with Napoleon and his collective after the Prussians were beaten back in the first campaign of the War of the Fourth Coalition. In response to the Confederation of the Rhine, several European powers again banded together to fight the French, including Russia, Great Britain, Prussia, and Sweden. The coalition may have lasted only a year, but some of the major battles of the Napoleonic wars were fought.

The new coalition was started by the ambitious Prussian king, Frederick William III, who believed his army to be capable enough to face the French without the backing of Russia, its biggest ally and neighbor. On October 8th, 1806, Napoleon started his invasion of Prussia with Louis-Nicolas d'Avout, one of his best generals and a Marshal of the Empire. The Prussian army was defeated by both generals in two different battles at Jenna and Auerstädt on October 14th. The total number of the French Army was 160,000, which defeated a vastly superior army of 250,000 in a matter of days, eliminating 25,000 and taking 150,000 as prisoners, one of the biggest losses for the anti-French coalition. On top of that, Napoleon also seized the Prussian artillery equipment and firearms, further bolstering his supplies without needing to call for more from home, which was already far behind. Berlin, which was then a part of Prussian territory, was occupied by October 27th, leading to a fast and stunning victory for the French forces in just nineteen days, the same amount of time Napoleon had to withstand a siege at Vienna a year before.

The next battlefront for Napoleon's army was Poland, where he ousted the Russian forces primarily with the assistance of the Polish and German forces, as well as the Dutch and the Italians in the Siege of Pomerania. The Polish campaign was total siege warfare on the battlefronts of Pomerania and Silesia. Even though Russia was one of the largest military powers of that time, the training and high morale that was present in Napoleon's peasant army, who worshipped him almost like a deity, was not present in their ranks, which allowed Napoleon to slowly but steadily beat the Russian armed forces throughout the rest of the year. After these sieges, Napoleon turned his gaze toward the Prussian capital of Königsberg in the early months of 1807. The Russian army retreated north after suffering one loss after another in the Battles of Eylau, Danzig, and Heilsberg throughout February, March, and June. Napoleon's final decisive victory against the Russians during the War of the Fourth Coalition was at Friedland, which forced the Tsar of Russia, Alexander I, to enter a peace treaty with Napoleon on July 7th at Tilsit. This peace treaty with the Russians formally ended the War of the Fourth Coalition, but the British were far from giving up.

Once the British saw that all of its allies of the Fourth Coalition had succumbed to defeat, it took it upon itself to wage a one-man tactical war to weaken Napoleon's naval power so that the French forces couldn't be as terrifying on the sea as it was on land. To this length, they engaged in the Gunboat Wars, the Finnish War, and the Dano-Swedish War, all between 1807 and 1809 before the formation of the Fifth Coalition against Napoleon's huge army.

In August 1807, the Royal Navy took the first initiative and attacked Denmark. Though Denmark was neutral up until this point, Napoleon's overwhelming influence in European politics and the newly formed peace with the Russian Empire was putting the country under political pressure to allow Napoleon use of its superb naval fleet, which posed a serious threat to the British navy if commanded by the brilliant tactician. The Danish capital of Copenhagen was laid under siege, and the Dano-Norwegian fleet was captured, allowing the British a safe route for trade as well as naval territory influence. After this turn of events, Denmark lost its war value to Napoleon because other than their fleet, the Danish had nothing to offer in terms of military strength and strategy. Despite this huge loss, the Danish stayed true to their French allies, conducting naval guerilla warfare against the British fleet and offering a small detachment of soldiers to aid France and Russia in their conquest of Sweden after the Emperors of France and Russia decided on banding together against the country to enforce the Continental System.

Napoleon conducted a two-pronged strike against Sweden, one via water and one via land. The campaign was led by Marshal Jean-Baptiste Bernadotte, one of Napoleon's best soldiers and generals, but the campaign was bought to a stalemate and instead became a series of border skirmishes, as the British navy prevented the French Army from crossing the Øresund strait, which separates Sweden from Denmark. Ultimately, the efforts of the British were all for naught as Russia and France divided Sweden amongst themselves at the Congress of Erfurt, which took place between September and October 1808. This turned Sweden into a French ally, something the British were trying to prevent through their invasion of Denmark. The naval guerilla warfare between Britain and Denmark lasted until 1812 with the British victory of the Battle of **Lyngør** where the last major Danish warship was sunk in combat.

The War of the Fifth Coalition

After the breakdown of the Fourth Coalition, there were no major political or military moves against France for about two years thanks to Napoleon's stupendous military victories as well as his alliance with Russia. Formed mainly by the British and the Austrians, the War of the Fifth Coalition brought in some significant changes that shook things up a bit for the Napoleonic Wars.

First, unlike the land-based warfare that had been going on since the French Revolutionary Wars, the focus of the war efforts was being driven toward naval warfare, which was ostensibly the gaping hole in Napoleon's otherwise superior military forces. While there were some notable land battles during the War of the Fifth Coalition, they pale in comparison to the warfare that was carried out at sea during this period. Britain made full use of its navy, and in a string of successful conquests, they managed to capture several French colonies.

Confident that its invasions after the end of the War of the Fourth Coalition had more than sufficiently weakened Napoleon's forces, the British tried to mount a rescue operation for the Austrians, who were taking heavy losses from the French forces, between July and December of1809 in the Walcheren Expedition. However, by a stroke of luck, it failed, although it was not due to military incompetence but due to a sickness known as the "Walcheren fever," which was later identified as malaria, that made most of the British soldiers sick and unfit for duty. With the arrival of Marshal Jean-Baptiste Bernadotte, who had recently been reinstated after being stripped of his position by Napoleon for disagreeing with the emperor, the French forces were led to fortify Antwerp, and the British forces soon realized it would be impossible for them to capture the French-controlled naval base. By the end of the British campaign, which had started with 40,000 men, 4,000 had died, and the rest spread the illnesses they contracted on foreign soil to the other units they were assigned to after the campaign was called off, except for a detachment of 12,000 soldiers. The British had finally learned the hard way that no matter how many naval victories they might win against the French at sea, on land the French were unbeatable, prompting them to take the bulk of the war to the water than face loss after loss of manpower and equipment through land warfare. Instead of a direct war of attrition, they developed the strategy of conquering French colonies and disrupting Napoleon's trade and supply routes, effectively weakening his army from within.

Napoleon's superior land artillery units held no advantage over the British ships as they had a clear view of the coast. Whenever the French troops tried to set up their artillery gear, the Royal Navy easily bombarded them from a distance, making it impossible to tear through the naval blockades, unless those who collaborated with the British were inexperienced, like the Spanish. Spain was one of the few countries that openly disliked the Continental System and sustained smuggling operations with Britain to carry on viable commerce that did not stress their economy. The French were aware of this, and at one point in 1808, Napoleon had invaded Spain and instituted a puppet monarch by placing his brother Joseph on the Spanish throne, which spread rebellion and dissent among the Spanish that the French found hard to put down. This was Napoleon's plan from the beginning, but in the end, it cost him dearly in terms of men and resources, not to mention the constant British interference that was already in place. The British were very good at espionage, which is how they acquired their numerous colonies in the first place, and they put this into good use to support the Spanish rebels. The Spanish slaughter in 1808, commonly known as the Second of May in which hundreds of civilians died, unified the Spanish even further instead of terrorizing them into silence. This event is thought to have officially begun the Peninsular War.

Putting down a rebellion on one's own turf is one thing, but to do so in a foreign land is another. It was very difficult, and it took its toll on the French Army. Due to Napoleon's concentration on the Rhine front, he left his eastern defenses pretty empty, with only about 170,000 men under General Berthier. The Austrians, seeing this as a golden opportunity, started engaging in skirmishes to win back Austerlitz, but they were put down shortly after at the Battle of Raszyn in April 1809. However, the Spanish invasion turned out to be the beginning of a series of bad decisions by the French central command, which was basically Napoleon himself. The British had successfully armed the Spanish insurrection, and the ensuing warfare between the rebels and the French forces saw a great loss in French numbers and resources. At first, Napoleon wasn't present in Spain, but once Madrid was taken over by the rebels, and the emperor made his way to the Spanish battlefront, successfully retaking Madrid and making the British withdraw for a short period of time until the Battle of Corunna on January 16th, 1809, when Napoleon left for the eastern front, leaving orders for Soult to deal with the British. Just like in the previous campaign, Soult again showed his aptitude by aggressively fighting the British.

Lieutenant-General Sir John Moore led a British detachment to aid the Spanish, but by the time he reached them, Madrid had already been retaken, prompting him to retreat. Napoleon ordered Soult to chase the retreating British army, which cornered their forces onto the island of Corunna, where the historic battle took place after a long chase with a lot of casualties for the British on the way. Soult chased the British with aggression that could be best described as dogged. In a matter of 10 days, he made his army march more than 200 miles in the hopes of overtaking the British, with the whole chase lasting 450 miles in total. Once they reached Corunna on January 11th, the British army found that the transport ships promised beforehand weren't there; instead, a handful of warships known as ships of the line and a few naval vessels were there, requiring them to hunker down and wait for three days, time which they couldn't afford over their hasty and troublesome retreat from Napoleon's army. That army began arriving the next day but refrained from attacking, which allowed the British army to recover a bit.

General Soult arrived with his artillery units on the evening of the 14th and started his assault on Corunna just as the sick and wounded were almost finished being loaded onto the British transport ships along with all carriable weaponry. Rather than letting the equipment they brought for the Spanish fall into the French Army's hands, they preferred to destroy all of it, which included a huge store of gunpowder, ammunition, and mortars. At first, it seemed that the British had the upper hand, due to their boosted morale and superior numbers, but General Soult's artillery units blew through their defenses, slowly moving from the lower ground to the higher ground where the transportation defenses had been placed on a ridge as per Moore's defensive plan. Soult had little intention of using cavalry as the terrain was too unsuitable for mounted battle, so he made the most out of his artillery, pushing the British back to the town of Elvina, where the British forces suffered immense casualties and lacked leadership for most of the battle. As night fell, the British army took advantage of the darkness to slowly fall back to their transport ships and retreat, since holding their ground was pointless and had already taken its toll. They kept the French fooled long enough by a densely populated front line which covered the retreat of the rear. When Soult realized that he had been tricked, he ordered artillery guns to be placed on the northern ridge of the harbor and to fire on the retreating ships. His attack successfully sunk four ships before the ships fired back, sailing out of their artillery range.

That was about all the success that came out of the Spanish conquest, though. After Napoleon left Spain after hearing reports of the Austrian attack on the eastern French front, insurrections sparked again in Spain, this time in the form of guerilla warfare in the countryside, which the residing French Army found hard to handle. The Spanish conquest had cost France a lot of resources and manpower, which greatly weakened their army for a time. After the Battle of Aspern-Essling, which signaled Napoleon's first tactical defeat, Napoleon made his way back to the home front and commanded the weary army slowly as the Battle of Aspern-Essling had resulted in heavy losses, almost 20,000 in number. This happened when Napoleon and his army tried to force their way across the Danube only to be obstructed by the Archduke Charles' forces. The first day of the battle took place at the small villages of Aspern and Essling, villages which led to the bridge connecting to the other side of the Danube. A fierce battle took place throughout the whole day on May 21st with the Austrians in possession of the villages in the morning. By the end of the day, both armies held half of the village of Aspern in their possession while Essling remained under French control, thanks to the efforts of Jean Lannes.

But this was all a ruse for the Austrian army's plans. Since the pathway across the bridge was narrow, Archduke Charles intended to let a significant number of enemies across before attacking them while cutting them off from the main French force at the same time, which succeeded to a degree. On the second day of the battle, the action started at Essling, where Jean Lannes drove out Prince

Rosenberg's forces whom he had been resisting the previous day. In Aspern, the French had broken through the enemy ranks only to be flanked from behind. Meanwhile, Napoleon launched an attack on the Austrian center, with Lannes on the left wing. The Austrian line was broken through, but Archduke Charles brought up his last reserve, squashing what could have been a French victory. Aspern was lost, and to add insult to injury, the bridges that connected the two sides of the river were destroyed as well. Napoleon retreated for the time being, succeeding in his next attempt to cross the Danube in the Battle of Wagram. However, Napoleon lost one of his finest commanders, Lannes, who died after being wounded by a cannonball on the second day of the battle.

By a stroke of luck, the British had found a way to wage economic warfare on the French with their superior Royal Navy which Napoleon's infantry or artillery virtually possessed no threat to. They continued this economic war long enough for Napoleon's alliance with the Russians to be fractured. The Peninsular War, which had started in 1807 with the French invasion of Portugal, continued until 1814, where the initial objective of invading the Iberian Peninsula turned into a defensive war to protect the Spanish smuggling operations by the Royal Navy that spanned across sixty major battles and thirty sieges. It effectively drained France of much of its resources in a war that lasted almost six years, which was far longer than what the French had expected. However, the War of the Fifth Coalition eventually did end, doing so in October 1809 with the Treaty of Schönbrunn in Vienna.

The following year, Napoleon tried to improve his relations with the Austrians by marrying Marie Louise, Duchess of Parma, in hopes of suppressing future Austrian interference in his military campaigns which already had the economy of the great empire in tatters. For a year or two, things remained rather peaceful, and Napoleon governed the largest empire in Europe with relative peace until the ill-fated Russian campaign.

Chapter 7 – The Napoleonic Wars, Part 2

Even though Napoleon and Russian Tsar Alexander I signed a peace treaty between the two nations, it did not last long. After the Russians sided with the French, the British were left dumbfounded with their Swedish allies and found themselves waging a war against their former ally in the Anglo-Russian War, which lasted from 1807 to 1812. Poland was the only strategic military location for both the French and the Russians, which happened to be neutral in wars and intended to remain that way. Both Napoleon and Alexander strived to control Poland from their respective positions, which soured their alliance. The Continental System didn't do much to boost their relationship either, as it was hurting the Russian economy. As the relationship between the two empires weakened, the British proposed a new anti-French coalition to Alexander, which was carried out in secret under the tables at first before formally turning into the Sixth Coalition (this war wouldn't take place until after Napoleon had started his war with the Russians, though). Napoleon was now suddenly fighting multiple enemies on many fronts after a longer period of peace, but unlike previous campaigns, Napoleon lacked the knowledge of his enemies, and this disastrous campaign ended in perhaps his biggest defeat.

The Russian Campaign: The Beginning of the End

Combining with the above-mentioned factors is the fact that further conquests were needed to keep the giant French Empire running, both economically and systematically. Napoleon, at the height of his power in 1812, began his infamous campaign into Russia, which is considered to be the beginning of his downfall by many historians.

Napoleon started out in June with a total number of 650,000 units (270,000 of which were Frenchmen with the others being allies or soldiers from subject areas) in his La Grande Armée, as he anticipated this campaign to be the biggest in his career so far. Both sides had different names for this war once it got under way. For the French, this was the Second Polish War, while the Russians dubbed it as the Patriotic War. The Russians used their large landmass to fall back and retreat instead of standing their ground and fighting, knowing full well the capabilities of Napoleon's artillery and cavalry units which were the reasons for his continuous military successes since he made himself emperor. The Russians evacuated entire towns and villages while using scorched-earth techniques to deny Napoleon any resources, to weaken his supply chain, and to weaken his cavalry by denying the horses and oxen, which were used for transportation purposes, grazing pastures. The ultimate objective of the massive Russian retreat was to cut Napoleon off from having a centralized army and to instead have one that had to be scattered when winter came. At the same time, the legendary Cossack Cavalry units used guerilla tactics to chip away at the main column. In one attack, the French reportedly suffered the loss of 95,000 men in a week from the main column, and this was all before a major skirmish had taken place in the whole campaign.

During this early phase of Napoleon's invasion, the only major battle that occurred was the Battle of Smolensk, which took place between August 16th and 18th and showed how practical the Russian retreat strategy was even though it meant giving away large swaths of Russian soil to the French without shedding much blood. It was a small fortress city occupied by Prince Pyotr Bagration's Second Army and led by General Barclay de Tolly, who played a vital role in keeping the number of casualties as low as possible. The battle wouldn't have even occurred in the first place if the Russian high command hadn't pressured Barclay into an offensive with the French. They did this for two reasons: Barclay was a German, making him a foreigner whom the upper echelon didn't trust completely, and Tsar Alexander I was nervous and wanted to crush Napoleon's army as soon as possible to obtain his dominion over Poland. The overall effectiveness of the Russian offense was derailed due to poor communication, mistrust, and independent actions taken by the commanding officers who disobeyed direct orders, ultimately resulting in a failed invasion.

The Battle of Smolensk started with the minor battle of Krasnov on August 14th, a small town near Smolensk. Being fed false information about Napoleon's movements, Barclay left a small detachment at Krasnov while setting out to scout and ambush Napoleon's forces if possible. Instead, the reserves left at Krasnik were attacked by a French force of 20,000. But Napoleon's Marshals, Michel Ney and Joachim Murat, also showed equal ineptitude, which allowed the Russians to retreat successfully with their munitions and supplies intact. When this happened, Barclay was in Neverovski and initially planned to flank Napoleon, but Pyotr Bagration, the commander of the forces in the south, pointed out that Napoleon's army possessed immediate danger to the strategic position of Smolensk, which was also heavily populated with civilians. Understanding the situation, Barclay changed his war strategy while sending orders to Smolensk for evacuation. Finding the situation adverse, the Russian tsar left Barclay in charge of defending Smolensk. Since Napoleon's tactics were unclear at this point, Barclay opted to fortify and garrison the city instead of defending it from the outside, which was exactly the opposite of what Napoleon had forecasted, knowing the value of the heavy cannons, ammunition, and supplies located within the fortress. He expected the Russians to fight tooth and nail to preserve these resources, but instead, he found the entire city garrisoned, forcing him to use artillery fire to level the city. Barclay didn't bother with defending much after two of the suburbs of the fortress were taken; he destroyed every usable military resource in the fortress and abandoned it with the fleeing soldiers and civilians, allowing the French to capture the city by nightfall. The French artillery fire was overwhelming, and it is estimated that there was a total of 20,000 casualties in the two battles combined, one of the heaviest on the Russian side during Napoleon's invasion of Russia. However, unlike the Russians, Napoleon was at a disadvantage to gather more men and supplies.

This tactical retreat by the Russians continued for three months, and although Field Marshal Barclay de Tolly's tactics were actually working, he was stripped of his position to be replaced with Kutuzov, who had fought against Napoleon during the War of the Third Coalition. Kutuzov was just as far-sighted as his predecessor and continued retreating along with using the scorched-earth tactics that were now eroding the French Army from within. Finally, the stalemate broke on September 7th at the Battle of Borodino. This was the biggest skirmish of them all, occurring on the outskirts of Moscow and involving more than 250,000 men in total from both sides. The action took place mostly near the village of Borodino, a village slightly farther away from the town of Mozhaysk, where Kutuzov had prepared fortifications to prepare for the Russian army's last stand. Borodino's Raevsky redoubt became the capture-the-flag point of both armies, with men dying on both sides left and right fighting to gain control of it throughout the day. It is estimated that the Russians lost one-third of their manpower on that day alone due to the continuous artillery attacks conducted by Marshals Eugine, Ney and Davout, and the French also suffered huge losses, making Napoleon's logistical and intelligence problems more evident. It got to the point where he did not give a command to give chase to the retreating Russian army, which had become his customary habit since the War of the Third Coalition as a show of dominance to his enemies. This was mainly due to the Cossack raid that brought the legendary cavalry unit dangerously close to Napoleon's headquarters after Kutuzov decided to use this attack as a feint for the ongoing evacuation to distract Napoleon's attention. The Russians showed an indomitable spirit that day with Kutuzov leading them. His Imperial Guard could have easily pursued the retreating forces as it had seen no fighting in the battle, and according to historical experts, they could have caused significant damage to them. But caution gave way to arrogance, and the Russian army was able to retreat safely. This was a tactical retreat as the Russians had been evacuating the civilians from the city all day and furthermore released convicts who started to engage in vandalism and the attacks against the French forces. In total, the French had smaller numbers when it came to casualties when compared to the Russians—it is estimated that out of the 75,000 lives lost, 44,000 were Russian alone while the remaining were French. To quote historian Gwynne Dyer, the deaths in the Battle of Borodino and its aftermath were like "a fully-loaded 747 crashing, with no survivors, every 5 minutes for eight hours."[2]

Napoleon captured Moscow on September 14th, and he entered into peace talks with the Russians, expecting a surrender. However, Tsar Alexander I refused, leading Napoleon to retreat from Moscow after five weeks of holding the city. This event is historically remembered as the Great Retreat, and it proved to be as difficult as the battles the army faced. The oppressive Russian winter was something the soldiers were not used to, and combined with diseases running rampant through the ranks and the lack of supplies, a lot of the French Army did not make it home.

The Great Retreat also proved to be disastrous since, on his way back home, Napoleon tried to capture Kaluga for resources and supplies, which ended up becoming the beginning of the Battle of Maloyaroslavets. The spirited and well-equipped Russian army forced Napoleon to change his retreat strategy, playing right into Field Marshal Kutuzov's plan.

The attack on Kaluga began with Napoleon's stepson, Eugène de Beauharnais, leading the advance toward the city with an army of 20,000. Kutuzov believed it to be a small foraging party from scout reports and decided to send a small unit of 15,000 cavalry and infantrymen with 84 guns to ambush them under General Dmitry Dokhturov. When General Dokhturov realized the propensity of the threat after he found the French already engaged in the town and having captured the bridgehead, he decided to hold a defensive position at Maloyaroslavets until General Raevski arrived with an additional 10,000 infantrymen. Kutuzov arrived the next day, and a fierce battle started which saw the Franco-Italian forces winning, despite the arrival of support. The Russian army eventually retreated, but they had achieved a strategic victory by forcing the French general to follow the route through Smolensk to return to France after this encounter, which would place him right in the middle of the harsh Russian winter without equipment and supplies in areas that had already been ravaged by the scorched-earth tactics used previously in the campaign. To add to his problem, guerilla attacks from local militias kept thinning the French Army into something that couldn't even be compared to its former glory when it had first set out with visions of riches and glory on the Russian campaign. The campaign formally ended when the last of the French soldiers left Russia on December 14th,1812, after crossing the Berezina River.

Napoleon came back with only 27,000 able-bodied soldiers, with 380,000 men dead or missing and 100,000 captured. The Russians lost around 210,000, a number that was a lot less than that of the French Army, and due to their shorter supply lines, the numbers were quickly replenished. Once the whole of Europe saw the French military on its knees and Napoleon thoroughly humiliated, it didn't take long for many of France's enemies to form a new coalition to finally bring down Napoleon.

The War of the Sixth Coalition

Soon after Napoleon's return to France, almost all of the countries involved in the previous coalitions formed the Sixth Coalition. This included Austria, Prussia, Sweden, and several German states. Napoleon wasn't the kind of soldier to keep brooding, and he focused his attention into rebuilding his army to meet the growing threat that was soon to become the War of the Sixth Coalition. Within 2 months of his return from Russia, Napoleon amassed a large army of 400,000, which was more than enough to defend the French Empire under Napoleon's command—or so the great commander thought. The War of the Sixth Coalition is considered to be the fall of Napoleon before his last attempt at the end of his life to retake his former power and glory. Faulty tactics, indecisiveness on the battlefield, the lack of intelligence, and the incompetence of one of his most trusted Marshals of the Empire, Michel Ney, who had accompanied him on his initial campaigns against the Coalition armies, all helped to attribute to Napoleon's downfall by the end of the War of the Sixth Coalition. Another big reason was his lack of a proper cavalry, which had played a large role in his successful campaigns earlier.

At first, it seemed that Napoleon had the upper hand, defeating the incoming Russian army, which had launched a counterattack on France after replenishing its army, and the Prussians at the Battle of Lützen on May 2nd, 1813, and the Battle of Bautzen, which took place between May 20th and 21st. Napoleon managed to inflict40,000 casualties on the Coalition forces. Even though he was victorious in these battles, Napoleon's rule and influence was reduced to the borders of France after his brother, Joseph Bonaparte, lost the Battle of Vitoria in June of 1813, as Napoleon had neither the manpower nor the resources to maintain the other sister republics he had created to expand French dominion. On August 13th, 1813, Napoleon set out across the Rhine to defeat the Coalition forces before they had enough time to unite and band against him.

In the Battle of Lützen on May 2nd, 1813, the Prussian army had the advantage as Russian Field Marshal Wittgenstein and Prussian Count von Blücher had 73,000 men in reserve on Napoleon's right flank, which Napoleon wasn't aware of due to faulty intelligence. This allowed the joint Russian and Prussian forces to retreat successfully, inflicting more casualties on Napoleon's army than they received all throughout the battle; overall, it was a strategic loss for the Coalition armies. The main battle took place when Marshal Ney, who was at the forefront, was suddenly ambushed. He ordered Ney to withdraw to Lützen, sending Ney reinforcements which took up defensive positions around the villages surrounding the city. Once they were ready, the rest of Ney's forces would retreat toward them, luring the Coalition forces to attack, which is when Napoleon would lead the main section of the French Army, which was 110,000 strong, in a counterattack against the enemy.

The plan worked perfectly at first as the two Coalition generals took the bait and concentrated their efforts on Ney, but the concealed 73,000 Coalition forces on the right upset Napoleon's plan. They laid a counterattack, forcing Napoleon's forces to come to a halt which allowed the main army engaged with Ney to retreat once the enemy commanders understood the French general's true intentions. The Coalition forces lost around 11,500 men (approximately 8,500 Prussians and 3,000 Russians), while Napoleon sustained a loss of between 19,500 and 22,000 soldiers, which was more than he had expected to lose.

Eighteen days after this first major battle of the War of the Sixth Coalition, the Battle of Bautzen took place between 20 and 21st May. After retreating from the Battle of Lützen, Generals Wittgenstein and Blücher were ordered to stop in their retreat at Bautzen by their respective rulers. Napoleon had 115,000 soldiers left after the last battle, while the Coalition forces of Russia and Prussia stood nearly 100,000 strong. Though Napoleon won a strategic victory in this battle, his main objective of destroying the enemy forces to render them incapable of carrying any further warfare failed due to the ineffective command of Marshal Ney.

Napoleon initially started with an artillery bombardment on the entrenched Coalition positions, who had formed into two defensive lines to withstand Napoleon's attack. These positions became compromised, however, and the Coalition forces were on the brink of defeat without an opening to retreat, just as Napoleon wanted. Unfortunately left an opening in the left flank with his aggressive attacks on the enemy on the other two sides. He repeated the same mistake the next day, capturing the village of Preititz instead of cutting off the Coalition forces, once again allowing the enemy to retreat. Both sides sustained heavy losses, though, with the French losing between 20,000 and 22,000 and the Prusso-Russians losing between 11,000 and 20,000. Despite the French winning Bautzen, the bulk of the Coalition forces safely got away, throwing a monkey wrench in Napoleon's plans.

On June 2nd, the Coalition leaders requested for a two and a half month's armistice known as the Armistice of Pleischwitz, which Napoleon was forced to accept due to failing his tactical objectives in his last two battles as well as the uncertainty in enemy intelligence and lack of manpower. Napoleon hoped to regroup his army properly and gain intelligence on his enemies, but in the end, it was the Coalition that gained the upper hand thanks to the armistice. The British were not officially a part of the coalition, but they had no need to be since they had been waging the Peninsular War against Napoleon since 1807. Around the time Napolcon signed the armistice with the Coalition forces, the British had launched the Salamanca campaign to create pressure on Napoleon's forces. This was the last vestige of control the French Army had over the region as the Anglo-Portuguese forces pushed them behind the Pyrenees in one skirmish after another by 1813 over a period of two months. At this time, the Austrians also joined the Russians and the Prussians, seeing an opportunity to get back at the French, making the Allied force strong and numerous with over a million in total in the German war theater alone. Napoleon, on the other hand, had amassed an army of about 650,000; the French Army was now standing almost as strong numerically as it had been when it set out for the Russian campaign the previous year. With the retreating forces from the Spanish front, his total army now stood at 900,000, considerably weaker than his Coalition counterparts for the first time since the start of the Napoleonic Wars. Of this total number, however, Napoleon could count on only half of them for total allegiance as many of the summoned forces were now on the verge of defecting to the Allies, tired of the constant wars that defined the Napoleonic regime. On top of that, the Coalition was conducting the German campaign where they were breaking up the divided German confederacies installed by Napoleon, which also made up a sizeable bulk of his military might. However, one tactical advantage Napoleon regained during the armistice was his cavalry units comprised of cuirassiers and dragoons which would bring him his unexpected victory at the upcoming Battle of Dresden, despite the sheer difference in numerical strength between the French and the Coalition armies.

After the armistice period was over in August, the first conflict that took place was the Battle of Dresden where Napoleon's smaller army won an overwhelming victory over the Coalition army's superior numbers. However, it was a strategic defeat for them as they kept with the Trachenberg Plan, which was named after where a conference took place during the armistice. The plan called for avoiding direct conflict with Napoleon and destroying his army by either defeating or strategically outwitting his comparatively inexperienced army and commanding officers, who were not the veterans Napoleon had amassed slowly over his decade-long conquest in various successful campaigns as he had lost most of them before or during the Russian campaign. Jean Baptiste Bernadotte, who was now Crown Prince Charles XIV John of Sweden, was an ex-Marshal of Napoleon's whose disapproval of Napoleon's methods got him stripped again of his military status. He knew exactly how Napoleon schemed and strategized. Count Radetzky von Radetz also helped Bernadotte a lot, which allowed the Allied army to properly outmaneuver Napoleon successfully for the first time in his career.

Before the Battle of Dresden, which took place between August 26th and 27th, Napoleon ordered the capture and fortification of the town, which was an important strategic point in the German war theater. He hoped to cut off the Coalition forces from their supply lines and to strike the main blow on the enemy forces when they would begin focusing their attack on the town. Instead, the Coalition forces engaged Napoleon's commanders in the Battle of Großbeeren, where Crown Prince Charles of Sweden defeated his former comrade Marshal Charles Oudinot in battle, striking a severe blow to Napoleon's strategic command. Marshal Blücher of Prussia shortly followed with his own victory over Marshal Jacques MacDonald at the Battle of the Katzbach, which also happened to be one of the largest conflicts of the Napoleonic Wars, engaging over 200,000 men in total for 5 straight days, ending with the main battle on August 26th, 1813. The Battle of Dresden also started on the same day as the Battle of the Katzbach when Karl Philipp, Fürst zu Schwarzenberg of Austria, Francis II of the Holy Roman Empire, Alexander I of Russia, and Frederick William III of Prussia all moved together to attack Marshal Saint-Cyr's corps. Observing the Coalition movements, the French began their fortifications for the upcoming battle as they waited for Napoleon to arrive to direct the flow of the battle. The general himself broke through the Coalition forces with a timing that was unexpected, recovering almost all of Saint-Cyr's position by nightfall. The following day, Napoleon won another skirmish on the left flank, defeating the Allied army's superior numbers in a brilliant victory. The rainy, damp weather of the battlefield worked to Napoleon's advantage when the Coalition armies were unable to fire their muskets, causing a huge number of casualties by the French cavalry, which was headed by Marshal Joachim Murat, who was responsible for the capture of 13,000 soldiers. But the enemy had eluded Napoleon again, instead of giving him the total decisive victory which he so desperately wanted.

Two days later, the Battle of Kulm took place, which lasted between August 29th and 30th. This battle signaled the second defeat for the French during the War of the Sixth Coalition when General Dominique Vandamme approached the town under Napoleon's orders to intercept the retreating Coalition forces, which resulted in heavy losses on both sides and an ultimate defeat for Vandamme's forces.

The Battle of Kulm was a tipping point in the war; if General Vandamme succeeded in garrisoning Kulm, the Coalition forces would be trapped between the two French armies. Initially, the Coalition army took up a defensive position as General Vandamme attacked the town, but by an unexpected twist of fate, help arrived for the fortified Coalition forces on the second day of the battle when Prussian forces, under the command of Friedrich von Kleist, tore through the French Army's rearguard, taking a decisive and important victory that would determine the fate of Napoleon's grand plans.

If the Battle of Kulm was the battle that tipped the scales, then the decisive battle of the War of the Sixth Coalition had to be the Battle of Leipzig, also commonly known as the Battle of the Nations since almost all of the major European countries took part in this epic and historic war that shaped the history of Europe for the next 100 years. The battle started on the October 16th, 1813, and continued until October 19th. This is considered to be the largest battle in of Europe prior to World War I, and it involved 600,000 soldiers and 2,200 artillery units, with the total number of casualties standing at 127,000.

The Coalition forces had a combined 380,000 troops at their disposal with 1,500 artillery guns. The French emperor, on the other hand, was outnumbered in every way, starting from his core army of 160,000 soldiers, which was mostly made of inexperienced soldiers.

He also had almost half the artillery power of his enemies. However, combining his forces with that of his Italian, Polish, and German allies, Napoleon's army stood at 225,000, which made the difference in numbers a bit better.

The Battle of Leipzig took place near the Pleisse and Parthe Rivers, which offered his numerically inferior forces the luxury of shifting sectors easily among the four land areas divided by the intersection of the two rivers. The excessive number of the Allied armies wouldn't allow them to pursue the same strategy as well. Another advantage that was ultimately of no use to Napoleon was the difference in opinions regarding the general battle tactics in the Coalition command, which was made up of Tsar Alexander I of Russia, King Frederick William III of Prussia, and Emperor Francis I of Austria. The Russian and Austrian monarchs couldn't agree on a battle strategy at first, and unbelievable as it might seem, they each carried out their own individual battle strategies. The prime bone of contention regarding their disagreement was the initial decision to attack Napoleon's position from both sides, which was drafted by the veteran tacticians of the Coalition, Prince Volkonsky of Russia, Gerhard von Scharnhorst of Prussia, Johan Christopher Toll of Sweden, and Karl Friedrich von dem Knesebeck of Prussia. The plan involved a simultaneous two-pronged attack from the left and right flank on Napoleon's supply base, which the Russian tsar rejected, pointing out that it didn't allow for flanking maneuvers as well. So, the commanders decided to divide the battlefield, with the Russian monarch choosing the north and the rest of the Coalition forces taking care of the south side. Although Alexander was more inexperienced in the matters of warfare, which the Russian monarch didn't like to admit, what he forecasted as being the loophole in the Coalition plans proved to be true, resulting in a drawn-out conflict in the south while his own forces followed a different plan executed by Blücher. The Russians' plan played out rather well, which was entrenching themselves in defensive positions at Möckern and Lindenau, and they saw a huge success in stopping the French from taking over Guilden Gossa, an important strategic position on the south side where the Coalition forces were fighting tooth and nail.

With the forces divided, the main conflict began, which was one of the bloodiest in European history in the pre-World War era. Battles were fought at multiple fronts due to the topographical division of the landmass. On the first day of the war, most of the action had been concentrated near Dolitz, Markkleeberg, Liebertwolkwitz, Möckern, Lindenau, and Wachau. The Austrian and Prussian action at Dolitz and Markkleeberg ended in losses for the French, while the Russian attack in the south at Wachau ended in failure as the French took the joint Russian and Prussian forces by surprise. However, Blücher had tremendous success at Möckern, eliminating the French forces and resistance there completely. The action at Lindenau cut off Napoleon from the troops he badly needed to attack the main body of the enemy as he instead bolstered the defenses at Lindenau, which hurt the French Army in the larger picture, proving that Alexander I's intuitions were correct and that keeping Napoleon's forces divided and separated was the best course of action.

Seeing the results of the first day of the battle and the logic in the Russian monarch's perspective, Schwarzenberg drafted a new plan which divided the forces into individual groups with individual tasks independent of one another to both attack Napoleon and cut off his way of retreat while ensuring there was a vast amount of reserves in case Napoleon had hidden reinforcements, a tactic which had aided in most of the Coalition victories so far. The Russian cavalry and Imperial Guard, along with the Austrian Imperial Guard, were sent to the town of Rotha as a reserve, while grenadiers and cuirassiers of the Austrian army were to march along the river to disrupt Napoleon's army with Blücher approaching Napoleon's position from the north with his forces.

On the second day, there were only two major skirmishes with both sides waiting for reinforcements to join them. The Coalition forces were replenished by a superior force of 145,000 while Napoleon only had 14,000 arrivals. The French Army suffered during both of the major skirmishes of the day, the first one being at the village of Gohlis where Napoleon's Polish allies were stationed. The attack was led by Russian General Sacken. The second skirmish was between the cavalries of the two armies, which were General Lanskoy's Russian 2nd Hussar Division and General Arrighi's III Cavalry corps. Lanskoy was ordered by Field Marshal Blücher, who had been promoted due to his immense success the previous day, and they attacked the French cavalry under the command of General Arrighi's III.

On the third day of the battle, October 18th, the French monarch sent an armistice proposal through General von Merveldt, who had been captured on the first day of the Battle of the Nations. Naturally, the monarchs declined the armistice and began the process of encircling the French Army. Most of the action of the third and penultimate day of the battle was focused around Probstheida, Paunsdorf, and Schönefeld. The bloodiest and fiercest skirmish took place in Probstheida, where General Barclay de Tolly's forces were marching to besiege the town. The French fought back fiercely, and with their well-fortified defenses, they had the advantage as well. The Prussian jägers took the initiative of the charge but were beaten badly by the French. However, three subsequent assaults took place after this, which thoroughly drained the French force's supplies as well as reduce their numbers dramatically. And while the action that took place in Paunsdorf and Schönefeld was not as fierce as the one in Probstheida, the action was heavier. Throughout the day, a lot of Napoleon's allies deserted him, causing swift French defeats at Paunsdorf and Schönefeld. The Swedish army also took part in the final fray under Crown Prince Charles, Napoleon's former Marshal whose jägers showed a valiant display with a minimal loss of 121 men. By dusk, the French Army, once feared and revered all across Europe, started its desperate retreat to France in a miserable state of affairs along with Napoleon.

A select few of Napoleon's Marshals, including Oudinot, MacDonald, and Józef Antoni Poniatowski, a Polish prince who was promoted to Marshal on the eve of the retreat, covered the retreat of the French Army, which started withdrawing from all major positions in the dark of the night until the next day. This was an order they carried out valiantly until the bitter end of the war the next day, October 19th. The Coalition armies, once they learned of the retreat, showed no mercy, perhaps due to the fact that they had suffered tenfold at the hands of his army for nearly two decades. Leipzig still had considerable defenses which were fortified by the remaining Marshals, which made reaching the bridge by which the French Army was retreating difficult for the Coalition forces, despite being the clear victors of the Battle of Leipzig. Marshal Oudinot's forces, numbering 30,000, planned to fight to their deaths on the streets if need be to protect the French retreat.

Napoleon's retreat continued fairly smoothly until a case of miscommunication in the French chain-of-command occurred coincidentally, costing the retreating French Army dearly. The order for demolishing the bridge passed from General Dulauloy to Colonel Montfort to a corporal. This corporal didn't have many vital details of the order, including the timing of the explosion. So, the hasty corporal blew the bridge around 1 p.m., killing thousands of French soldiers and allowing thousands to be captured in the panic and confusion that ensued. This hasty detonation also cut off Oudinot's retreat in joining the main forces by nightfall. Oudinot managed to swim across the river, but he was one of the lucky few as many drowned while attempting to cross the river. This also marked Napoleon's loss of his last allies, Denmark and Norway.

After the shameful retreat, Napoleon was no longer the feared military figure that he once was. Tsar Alexander I took this opportunity to instigate the other members of the Coalition to take the war to France and finish off Napoleon once and for all. The Coalition armies chased the retreating French, only to be stumped at Hanau, where, the army of the Kingdom of Bavaria attempted to ambush the French, who put up a fierce fight for four days inflicting heavy losses on the Coalition forces, allowing the French forces and

Napoleon more than enough time to retreat back to France. Back in France, Napoleon knew full well what was coming and started preparing for the upcoming Coalition attacks on French soil. The backbone of his peasant force was lost, however, and the French forces were in tatters.

In March 1814, the Coalition began its invasion of France. The French Army was on the defensive now, with foreigners invading French soil, and in a series of defensive battles, the Coalition forces drove back the French to Paris, similar to the way the Allied forces made their way to Berlin in World War II. The Coalition forces took over Paris on March 30th, 1814, after a hard-fought Six Days' Campaign, which was Napoleon's last rally for defense against the Coalition. Though he won multiple major battles against the encroaching Coalition army, including the Battle of Champaubert, the Battle of Montmirail, the Battle of Château-Thierry, and the Battle of Vauchamps, using some of the most complex tactics in his career, it ultimately turned into an overall defeat once he ran out of supplies and tried to retreat to Fontainebleau to regroup. A week after the Allies took Paris, on April 6th, 1814, Napoleon finally realized that he had to face reality and abdicated. He was sentenced to exile on the island of Elba.

Napoleon's enemies had scored a huge victory which redrew the borders of the European map, but the effects of Napoleon's administrative principles, including the Napoleonic Code, lingered after his death for far longer. Once Napoleon was taken care of, the monarchy was reinstated in France, and Louis XVIII became the King of France, inheriting his brother's role as monarch prior to the French Revolution. Everything would have slowly shifted back to normal except for the fact that Napoleon decided to make another push for the power he thought he deserved. After serving ten months of his sentence, he started the final war of his career.

The War of the Seventh Coalition

The last of the Napoleonic Wars, the War of the Seventh Coalition, began after Napoleon escaped from Elba and made his way to Paris, collecting supporters on his way. Once he reached Paris, he deposed the recently restored king and reclaimed the crown for himself. This prompted the countries of the Sixth Coalition to band together against Napoleon again. After his coup, Napoleon mustered a force of 280,000, as well as the men that joined him during his march on Paris, and issued a draft of 2.5 million more soldiers, although it never came to happen. He also recalled what was left of the veterans of his previous campaigns as well. With this paltry force, he faced the Coalition forces, which numbered about 700,000 and which included the superior British navy, weary but still battle-ready, fresh from the Peninsular War that ended the year before.

Napoleon's first point of attack was Belgium, where he preemptively struck the Prussians with about 124,000 men, which led to the Battle of Ligny on June 16th, 1815. The first phase, like the prior war that led to his fall, was successful—Napoleon successfully pushed the Prussians and British out. Napoleon led the charge of his Armée du Nord (Army of the North) along with Marshal Michel Ney, who forced Arthur Wellesley, 1st Duke of Wellington, to fall back to a village a few miles south of Waterloo, which would come to be Napoleon's last great battle as well as the last battle of the War of the Seventh Coalition. Once both the British and Prussians had retreated, Napoleon ordered a mounted offensive on both the British and Prussians at the same time to stop them from regrouping.

But there was a problem with this plan. Unbeknownst to Napoleon, they were already regrouping at the village of Wavre. Marshal Emmanuel de Grouchy was tasked with routing the Prussians while Napoleon decided to chase down the British himself along with Marshal Ney. Marshal Grouchy's failure, due to Napoleon's miscalculations, was one of the main reasons for Napoleon's defeat at the Battle of Waterloo. Even though Grouchy was victorious at the

Battle of Wavre, the damage it caused to Napoleon's plans was not worth it. Not only did reinforcements fail to reach Napoleon in time, but the battle also allowed the Prussians to bolster and reinforce the British forces with 72,000 troops at the Battle of Waterloo.

Once Wellington was assured aid was coming from the Prussians, he stopped retreating and held his ground at the Mont-Saint-Jean escarpment, withstanding multiple French assaults before the beginning of the Battle of Waterloo. That fateful battle was fought on June 18th, 1815. Napoleon was facing the Prussian and British forces led by Wellington and Field Marshal Blücher, the man who is considered to be responsible for Napoleon's defeat in the battles of the War of the Sixth Coalition. Napoleon already had a hard time chasing Wellington's forces by land due to the bad weather that was making the ground slippery and difficult to walk on. Napoleon had a total of 48,000 infantrymen along with 14,000 cavalrymen, who were all experienced veterans of what remained of the army of his previous military campaigns. The cavalry units served their purpose well, due to the bad weather that was slowing down the infantry.

Before the Prussian reinforcements arrived, the coalition forces of the British and Prussians stood at 67,000, nearly the same number as Napoleon's army. But the problem was the coordination of the command. Wellington's commanders were not chosen by him, and the cavalry unit that he needed the most to face Napoleon's forces was under the Earl of Uxbridge, Henry Paget, who had authority from the Duke of York to pursue his own battle plans despite being Wellington's second-in-command. Fortunately, his Prussian allies were well organized and willing to coordinate with him, which led to the glorious Coalition victory at the Battle of Waterloo.

The battle started with Napoleon attacking Hougoumont, an estate house turned into a military outpost, which was occupied by the British. The initial French attack was met with suppressive fire from the British artillery, forcing the French to retreat and counter back with their own artillery. The attack started, according to some sources, around 11:30 a.m. and continued until the afternoon when

Napoleon ordered the house to be burned down and leveled after failing to capture it despite repeated assaults. According to Wellington's memoirs:

> I had occupied that post with a detachment from General Byng's brigade of Guards, which was in position in its rear; and it was some time under the command of Lieutenant-Colonel MacDonald, and afterward of Colonel Home; and I am happy to add that it was maintained, throughout the day, with the utmost gallantry by these brave troops, notwithstanding the repeated efforts of large bodies of the enemy to obtain possession of it.[3]

The battle was never meant to be that large, and many historians think it was actually meant to be a diversionary attack by Napoleon which spun out of control due to the ferocity with which the British defended it. This made Napoleon think it was a key point for winning the war, causing the French to divert their artillery resources there for the counterattack after they were initially beaten back. Wellington also did the same and fortified his artillery units to secure Hougoumont. When Napoleon spotted the approaching Prussian army which Grouchy was meant to keep away from Waterloo, it turned the tides of the battle against him. Napoleon charged forward, attacking the British and moving the lines of battle to La Haye Sainte, which was a farmhouse positioned at Charleroi-Brussels road in present-day Belgium, after making good use of his cavalry against Wellington's unruly second-in-command of Uxbridge, who led a cavalry charge from the rear of Napoleon's forces and might have brought in good results had he not acted independently against his commander's plans and formation.

While the British army was facing the brunt of Napoleon's attack, the Prussian and other British forces were making full use of the time available to them to get organized and rout Napoleon's forces from the rear, which proved to be effective. The Prussian IV Corps occupied Plancenoit at first, but General Lebou, under Napoleon's command, recaptured the village after fierce fighting that lasted until nightfall. While Napoleon's forces were busy with the skirmish at Plancenoit, the Prussian 1 Corps, led by General Zieten, flanked Napoleon's forces from the back, cutting off his way of retreat while joining forces with other units for the final assault. This propelled Napoleon to use his Imperial Guard, which he had been holding off as a reserve unit. This was the biggest skirmish in the Battle of Waterloo, and Napoleon led the Imperial Guard himself, arranging them into square formation battalions. Leading the assault was Ney whose incompetence, once again, was one of the major reasons for Napoleon's defeat at the Battle of Waterloo. At first, the battle was in a deadlock with both sides fighting fiercely without giving an inch, but General Chassé of the Dutch army finally broke the stalemate with overwhelming artillery fire conducted by Captain Krahmer de Bichin, breaking through the ranks of the 1st and 3rd grenadier divisions of the Imperial Guard on the left flank. The middle flank of the Imperial Guard soon faltered as well, as Ney was mounting a charge on the right flank instead of the middle as planned, leaving the middle flank without leadership. By the time Napoleon sent Colonel Crabbé to communicate with Ney and change the course of action, it was too late. The whole French Army was on the retreat.

The Battle of Waterloo ended in Napoleon's defeat, and he abdicated the throne once again. Louis XVIII was restored to the throne, and Napoleon was exiled once more, this time to Saint Helena, an island in the South Atlantic Ocean. He died there on May 5th, 1821, at the age of 51. The cause of his death has been debated over the years. Some believe he died of an ulcer or cancer, while others think he may have been poisoned by arsenic.

The end of the Battle of Waterloo and Napoleon's second abdication changed Europe's political scene for years to come, which we will discuss next.

Chapter 8 – The French Revolutionary Wars and Napoleonic Wars from a British Socio-Political Perspective

Much like its Asian counterpart of Japan, Britain is also an island nation, being separated from mainland Europe by the British Channel. As a result, its peaceful existence depended a lot on a chaotic mainland Europe so that the embers of war wouldn't reach their shores by many of the large European countries like Spain, Russia, or Portugal. These forces could crush the island nation easily if they allied together. The British navy was historically a strong deterrent for other countries to not meddle with them, but the nation was by no means impregnable. For this very reason, it had a vested interest in the French Revolutionary Wars from the very beginning of the French Revolution for two reasons—France was their major opponent, and a divided Europe would serve British interests well in European politics.

During the eve of the French Revolution in 1789, Europe hung on a delicate balance of power between the Ottoman Empire, Russia, Austria, the Bourbons, and the Habsburgs, which was shifted by the French Revolutionary Wars. Before then, Britain had no mainstay in the European political power struggle as it was isolated from the mainland. All of these major powers, aside from France, were embroiled in wars and were busy carving territories out of small countries like Poland, Bavaria, and Italy. But once the French Revolutionary principles spread out like wildfire across many of these feudal countries that had been groaning under the oppression of feudal monarchy for centuries, the theaters of war shifted rapidly, as many of these countries started aiding the French military to fight against these major political powers. This attributed to the early victories of France in the French Revolutionary Wars. The French were seen as heroes by many of these smaller countries, allowing the French to easily create sister republics and a revolutionary period in Europe that threw the whole continent into chaos. Meanwhile, the British were observing all of these world-changing events from a distance.

Even though the French Revolutionary Wars didn't reach the shores of Britain, the British monarchy despised the very thought of the newly found principles of revolution as they would be a great threat to their colonial power, which would prove to be a great threat to the British Empire that was only strong when combined with the trade power of their colonies. Thus, the British started providing support against the French, which they started openly doing during the War of the Second Coalition when they used their naval force to corner Napoleon along with many strategic naval points of France through their superior and powerful navy. This conflict later became the foundation of the Napoleonic Wars, which was temporarily halted after the Treaty of Amiens in 1802 when France and England were the only remaining key players of the War of the Second Coalition. This marked the beginning of the Wars of the Third, Fourth, Fifth, Sixth, and Seventh Coalitions that went on for a decade, from 1803 to 1815. All of these Coalitions were short-lived, with the British as the only common ties between them all. The British were shrewd and knew that in terms of sheer numbers they would be no match for Napoleon's military might, as his entire nation was a military machine by itself, churning out as many soldiers as Napoleon required as long he was achieving military glory and new territories. So, what the British did was constantly finance the military and political rivals of Napoleon to whittle down Napoleon's military might bit by bit. If an army lacked supplies, the British provided them with whatever requisitions they required, be it weapons, bullets, boots, or food supplies. The British supported military campaigns against France in every possible way, starting in the latter half of the French Revolution. The wars were also good for the British economy—an increasing number of armies and nations were starting to become dependent on British trade to support their civil structures, bolstering Britain's wealth, which then allowed them to generously fill the coffers of war during the Napoleonic Wars.

Chapter 9 – What Led to the Fall of Napoleon

While Napoleon was a shrewd and capable military officer, his arrogance at his successes made him too proud for his own good. It is true that as a warrior and a leader, he matured throughout the years, starting from his campaigns during the French Revolution to the many numerous wars waged during the Napoleonic Wars. But he made many miscalculations along the way, getting too greedy and making unnecessary enemies that he could have avoided had he been more level-headed. Most historians agree that his first political mistake was the betrayal of Spain and the enforcement of the Continental System on them. Setting his eyes on the Spanish territory abundant with supplies and loot was a terrible idea as the Spanish started their own rebellion akin to the French Revolution. Trying to engage an army that was accustomed to guerilla warfare instead of the open-field warfare that the French specialized in, Napoleon was forced to face long-term losses during his short Spanish campaign to quell the Spanish rebellion. This campaign also continued to drain French military resources during the whole stretch of the Peninsular War, a war which the British brilliantly won with their Spanish cohorts and superior naval power. Adding to that was his unnecessary cruelty and use of violence to subjugate his conquered lands, which angered many throughout his military career. For a man who preached and used the motto "Equality, Liberty, and Fraternity" to justify his wars and his role as a liberator instead of an invader, he took his price of granting liberty from the "liberated" regions by looting, plundering, and committing mass murders of prisoners and civilians, which many of his admirers hide in their books of his history.

To give one example of this, the following is Napoleon's written orders to a commander in Hesse who was quelling a revolt.

> My intention is that the main village where the insurrection started shall be burnt and that thirty of the ringleaders shall be shot; an impressive example is needed to contain the hatred of the peasantry and of that soldiery. If you have not yet made an example, let there be one without delay [...] Let not the month pass without the principal village, borough or small town which gave the signal for the insurrection being burned, and a large number of individuals being shot [...] Traces must be left in the cantons which have rebelled.

To be honest, though, this is not totally unexpected of a man who reached the heights of fame in the first place by shooting his own people and made nothing of it, later on referring to it as "firing a whiff of grapeshot" against unarmed protestors who were merely civilians.

His second biggest mistake, which is directly tied to his downfall, is the disastrous invasion of Russia which broke Napoleon's army so badly that it never returned back to its full efficiency in the following wars and skirmishes. Adding to that was the fact that his enemies had learned greatly from his many victories, which first became evident at 1809 in the Battle of Wagram. The Russians fed into his greed of capturing land and whittled down his army slowly as he went deeper and deeper into the heart of Russia, making his victory at Moscow a blank one since he could not occupy and control the invaded territories with the tired and broken army he had, causing him to ultimately retreat back to France in shame.

His third major mistake was immediately going back to war after the Russian campaign to face the Sixth Coalition instead of consolidating his power and renewing his allegiances with the sister republics he helped to create. These republics ultimately ended up betraying him at the end of the War of the Sixth Coalition. The strain on his treasury and the lack of dependable allies made short work of his political and military influence after his public defeat in Russia, which had shown Europe that Napoleon was not as invincible as they had made him out to be from his numerous past military victories.

His final mistake was not focusing his attention at home, which he had stayed far away from for most of the time during the Napoleonic Wars. His military victories pulled the public support on his side at home, but the French bourgeoisie, who facilitated his rise to power in the first place, were growing tired of Napoleon's war games, especially after the Russian campaign. This new elite class had originally intended Napoleon to be the man to cement their status and wealth and to legitimize their influence in society, which he did to a certain degree by instating the Napoleonic Code and reintroducing the Church back to mainstream society. However, war was a cruel mistress which emptied their pockets while Napoleon pursued his lofty ambitions with diminishing results. As a result, it didn't take long after Napoleon's first abdication for the bourgeoisie to readily accept Louis XVIII with a smile on their faces, understanding that the age of Napoleon was over and that only by supporting the new monarchy could they hope to retain their status and wealth which the new monarch would undoubtedly need in his new tenure.

Despite all the odds, the embers of the French Revolution never died out, and the newly formed class system put in place by Napoleon paved the way for modern capitalism, which spread across Europe during the historic period after the Napoleonic Wars which is known as "The Concert of Europe." In many ways, Napoleon's mistakes paved the way for the abolishment of feudalism that might not have been possible any other way. Each conquest undertaken by Napoleon was done under the banner of liberty, which ultimately planted the seeds of mass nationalist movements all across the territories Napoleon had occupied. So, in a way, his mistakes were blessings in disguise as they helped to shape the future of Europe in ways that intellectuals, monarchs, and ideologists of the time could not have predicted.

Conclusion

As stated multiple times before, the geopolitical scenario in Europe saw a radical change after the Napoleonic Wars, which was almost like the Italian Renaissance except the conditions were radically different. Many borders had to be redrawn as Napoleon fractured the continent of Europe. It was nothing like it had been before the start of the wars, and it was now split into smail confederacies and countries all screaming for freedom and independence, which can be attributed to the aftereffects of the French Revolution. But at the same time, alliances between many European countries were forged and old enmities were forgotten, which led to rapid technological and economic changes. The Napoleonic Wars forced countries to find new ways to churn out weaponry and other assets as efficiently as possible, leading to the Industrial Revolution, the true turning point of modern society. Most of the Rhine confederacies created by Napoleon under his rule subverted back to their original forms while others were consumed by the Coalition countries like Prussia. This allowed Prussia to become the new European superpower as it had obtained many new territories in the Rhine sector. But the biggest aftermath was the nationalism that arose, which overthrew monarchies and changed the way of life all over Europe by the First World War. In fact, it is nationalism that triggered World War I and did away with monarchy for good, not only in most of Europe but in many countries around the world as well. For instance, even though Napoleon never attacked Latin America, the Napoleonic Wars indirectly affected many Latin American countries. This mainly happened thanks to Spain and the interchange of ideas between intellectuals and revolutionaries of Spain and its Latin American colonies.

Hopefully, the reader now has a better understanding of Napoleon's conflict with the British, the French Revolution, and the overall circumstances that led to the continuation of the Napoleonic Wars. History has seen the rise and fall of many opportunists and warmongers, and Napoleon can be counted among them. While his military achievements were terrific and his contribution to tactics and strategy in warfare helped to shape modern warfare tactics and strategies, he also had his downsides. The main reason he is so revered even after historically being proven to be a cruel dictator and mass murderer is that the foundations of modern society are based on the social system principles he laid down, the idea of equality, liberty, and fraternity, as well as his being the brightest military mind of his time. The truth is, he used this doctrine as a weapon, much like religious leaders who still use religion to justify wars. Napoleon's antics also led to a weakened France, which never got back to its former glory as a European superpower due to being restricted in trade and political alliances and being mistrusted by most of its neighbors for a long time after his death.

However one might view him, there is no denying the fact that his actions of anarchy and chaos changed Europe as well as the modern world for what it is today. Whether one chooses to remember him as a military hero and tactical genius or a despot tyrant who used whatever he had at his disposal to justify an unending cycle of war to satisfy his lust for power is up to you.

Free Bonus from Captivating History (Available for a Limited time)

Hi History Lovers!

Now you have a chance to join our exclusive history list so you can get your first history ebook for free as well as discounts and a potential to get more history books for free! Simply visit the link below to join.

Captivatinghistory.com/ebook

Also, make sure to follow us on Facebook, Twitter and Youtube by searching for Captivating History.

Here's another book by Captivating History that you might be interested in

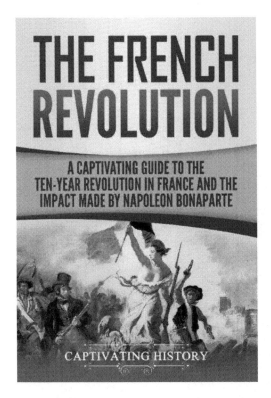

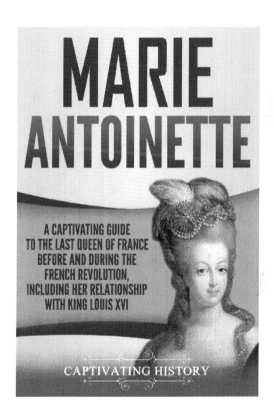

MARIE ANTOINETTE

A CAPTIVATING GUIDE TO THE LAST QUEEN OF FRANCE BEFORE AND DURING THE FRENCH REVOLUTION, INCLUDING HER RELATIONSHIP WITH KING LOUIS XVI

CAPTIVATING HISTORY

Made in the USA
Columbia, SC
07 July 2023

20156124R00064